La Casa Loca

GLOUCESTER MASSACHUSETTS

ROCKPORT PUBLISHERS

Latino Style Comes Home

La Casa Loca

45 Funky Craft Projects for Decorating and Entertaining

Kathy Cano-Murillo

First published in the United States of America by
Rockport Publishers, Inc.
33 Commercial Street
Gloucester, Massachusetts 01930-5089
Telephone: (978) 282-9590
Fax: (978) 283-2742
www.rockpub.com

Library of Congress Cataloging-in-Publication Data
Cano-Murillo, Kathy.
   La casa loca : Latino style comes home : 45 funky craft projects for decorating and entertaining / Kathy Cano-Murillo.
      p.   cm.
   ISBN 1-56496-943-6 (pbk.)
   1. Handicraft. 2. House furnishings. 3. Decoration and ornament—Latin America—Themes, motives. 4. Decoration and ornament—Mexico—Themes, motives. I. Title.
   TT157 .C218 2003
   745.5—dc21   2002014885

ISBN 1-56496-943-6

10 9 8 7 6 5 4 3 2 1

Design: Susan Raymond
Cover Image: Bobbie Bush Photography, www.bobbiebush.com
Photography: Bobbie Bush Photography, www.bobbiebush.com
Layout: Leeann Leftwich Zajas
Copyeditor: Pamela Hunt
Proofreader: Stacey Ann Follin

Printed in Singapore

Contents

.... .8

Introduction 12

GETTING STARTED 14
Latin Styles and Traditions . . . .
Materials and Techniques . . . .

HOME ACCESSORIES 18
Nifty *Nicho* Postcard Shrine 20
Fruit Crate Revolutionary Frame 22
Tree of Life Light-Switch Cover 24
Zoot Suit Night-Light 26
Foaming Flan Soap Bars 28
Fabric Wall Hanging 30
Reverse-Painted Box 32
Stamped Folk Art Boxes 34
Mirrored Mission Ornaments 36
Peso Picture Frame . . . .

GARDENING 40
Tin Plant Pokes 42
Aztec Cactus Garden 44
Glittery Soda Pop Vases 46
Mexican Cowgirl Wind Chime 48
Milagro Tree Ribbons 50
Spicy Candle Lanterns 52
Cigar Box Birdhouse and Feeder 54
Mexicali Mini-Lights . . . .

FIESTA 58
Frida Kahlo Fiesta Placemats 60
Flowered Balcony Gift Tower 62
Hot, Hot, Hot! Chips and Salsa Set 64
Tissue Flower Topiary . . . .

Dia de los Muertos Serving Tray 66

Mexican Margarita Candle 68

Festive Papier-Mâché Skull 70

Lucha Libre Place-Card Holders 72

Loteria Glass Charms 74

FURNISHINGS

Crazy for Carmen Miranda Lamp 78

Bossa Nova Barstool 80

Mexican Cinema End Table 82

Manic Hispanic Canvas Painting 84

Tamale Oja Wreath 86

El Sol Wall Shelf 88

Café Cultura Clock 90

Talavera Tile Treasure Mirror 92

T-Shirt Toss Pillow 94

PERSONAL ACCESSORIES

Bottle Cap Pebble Pins 98

Crazy Calaca Jewelry Set 100

Wood-Burned Retablo 102

Stained-Glass Prayer Candle 104

Divine Intervention Car Cross 106

Flashy Flamenco Box 108

Mariachi Tote Bag 110

Novela Note Cards 112

Embroidered Dish Towels 114

TEMPLATES 117

RESOURCES 126

CONTRIBUTORS 127

Introduction

It took 21 years, a pitcher of margaritas, and a boyfriend with an attitude for me to appreciate my Mexican-American heritage. Aside from eating my dad's tamales every Christmas, I never had the desire to indulge in anything related to my culture. It wasn't totally my fault—as a hip all-American chica growing up in the early '80s, I couldn't help it that my world revolved around techno tunes, fast food, kitschy shops, and European travel. I thought life was good.

I didn't have a clue as to what I was missing out on until I met him: Mr. Vato Loco—now known as my husband of 13 years. It was 1984, and he was decked out in a charcoal-gray zoot suit, a shiny pair of Stacey Adams shoes, and a pristine 1948 Chevy. Based on my perception of cool at the time, I should have been appalled. Instead, my heart skipped a beat when he asked me out.

On the way to our first dinner, I giggled when I confessed I had never so much as tasted a taco. He shook his head in shame when I confessed I'd rather be caught singing in the shower than listening to mariachis. Much to my horror, he responded by pulling right up to a Mexican restaurant. As it turns out, it was May 5th.

"Today is Cinco de Mayo, Kathy," he said, as he looked me sternly in the eye. "You are going to eat Mexican food tonight, and you are going to like it! You should be proud of your ancestry, and I'm going to make sure you are before the night is over!" I was so offended. But more than that, I was secretly thrilled. By the end of el noche, I became an Aztec princess—OK, maybe a klutzy, nerdy one, but the fire was ignited nonetheless. I experienced my first chimichanga platter, belted out a corrid with a mariachi trio, and even discovered I had a natural talent for Latin dancing. After a couple margaritas, I was rolling my rrrr's with the best of them. That experience was the salsa on the tortilla chip that was my life.

Afterward, I couldn't get enough of my Mexican–American culture. After almost 20 years, I'm still embarrassed at my early ignorance and have since devoted all my energies to absorbing all I missed. Aside from tasting, read-ing, touching, dancing, learning, singing, teaching, and breathing all things Latin, Mexican, Chicano, and Hispanic, I found a way to turn my negative into a positive. My exuberant passion exploded into multicolored glitter! Viva!

For more than a decade, my husband and I have designed what we call Chicano folk art, which keeps the flames burning in our house and hearts. We are most happy when we can add spicy visual flavor to anything we can—from our office supplies and bedrooms to our cars and clothing. Sure, the bright colors and varnish can have a dizzying effect at times, but to us, it's worth it.

This book is a compilation of the most maravilloso ideas of what we've come up with, and then some. Sharing these projects with you is my way of spreading the beauty, fun, and uplifting spirit that I have come to know and love.

I call it La Casa Loca. After reading this book, I think you will understand why. However, the only thing you won't find here is a pitcher of margaritas. You'll have to fend for yourself on that one.

Whether you are an expert or a novice, the following pages will serve as a basic guide. You'll find that La Casa Loca lightly touches on a range of topics that pertain to the projects—just enough to ignite your creativity flame. Mexican music and munchies are not required, but they are certainly recommended for keeping the mood festive!

Getting Started

So what exactly does La Casa Loca mean? The actual translation is "The Crazy House," but within these pages, it refers to changing the ordinary into extra-ordinary and the bland into bright. Think of an overabundance of mucho colores, in hues of red, green, yellow, purple, and blue strategically placed anywhere a paintbrush can fit. That is the closest definition you'll find here of La Casa Loca.

Now it's time for your own version, with a little inspiration from the following projects. This book is all about livening up your living space with a splash of Latino art and culture. It will pep up not only your decor but your mood as well. Here you will discover an exploded piñata of playful patterns and textured celebrations in which to Latin-ize your own casa. Nothing can top the look and feel of imported Mexican furniture and accessories, but who says you can't add a few dashes of whimsy and spice of your own?

Whether your style is campy or classy, if you have a soft spot for South of the Border decor, you'll raise a shot glass to the infusion of traditional motifs with contemporary crafting. La Casa Loca will allow you to use ordinary Mexican nov-elties for anything, except what they were originally meant for. Rather than play Loteria (Mexican bingo), you'll cut up the game for decoupage projects. Kitschy retro album covers that are usually buried in a record collection will become the sassiest tote bags on the beach. And you might as well stop tossing out the Corona bottle caps now, because you'll need them for a fabulous abstract art object for your cantina-inspired patio.

Inspired yet? Read on and you will be. No translation dictionary required.

Latin Styles and Tradition

Ay dios mío! How can one accurately define Latin style? Before visions of a sleeping man in a sombrero sitting by a cactus or a string of chili pepper lights pop in your head, read on. Those stereotypes are everything Latin style is not. What it does happen to be is any or all of the following: diverse, rustic, shiny, colorful, exotic, robust, dramatic, flamboyant, evocative, proud, humorous, spiritual, and so much more.

The term "Latin" is as broad as a Friday-night Mexican food buffet. Before you reach for an artsy antacid, relax. La Casa Loca keeps it simple by honing in on the aspect of the art and design of Latin style. The best part is you don't even have to speak Spanish.

Cubano, Mexicano, Puerto Rican, Nuyorican, Spanish, Chicano, Bolivian, Brazilian, Guatemalan, and so many other ethnicities can be mixed and matched to culturally converge under one vibrant umbrella. Although each region has its own savvy signature, such as the Spanish flamenco dancers or striped Guatemalan fabric, the universal thread of crafty cleverness unites them all. The thought should induce romantic images from old world Europe to tribal scenes of Central and South America that are weighted with pre-Columbian influences.

A common example of Latin style at its best (next to the real thing) is in the homes in the Southwest region of the United States. Using Mexico and Spain as the inspirational foundation, these houses have walls that sport stucco or faux finishes in rich, bold tones and are trimmed with Talavera tiles. The floors are lined with either Saltillo tile or painted concrete. The furnishings are chunky and oversized, and the accent pieces include painted tin candlesticks, coconut masks, wood-block prints, red clay patio chimneys, and bright baskets. The tones range from earthy to glossy and contemporary to primitive.

No matter what aspect of Latino life lights your fire, there are ways to harness it for use as an expressive twenty-first-century art form. One example is the ancient Aztec calendar. It was created centuries ago as a means of foretelling the future. These days, the circular collage is used in the form of concrete wall hangings, elaborate T-shirt designs, jewelry pieces, and even as company logos. No matter what the fashion, the original intention holds true, whereas its imagery doubles as a stunning conversational showpiece.

But it's much more than just a colorful calendar on the wall. Latin style is a gregarious way of living that is woven, painted, carved, sketched, punched, sewed, and chiseled every minute into holidays, meals, and family gatherings. Think hot hues on floor rugs or party favors, scrumptious food dishes embellished with searing chilies, centerpieces layered with ornate hand-punched tin, and rows upon rows of *papel picado* (Mexican paper cutting) banners hanging from the ceiling. Whether it's a solo piece or an outlandish combo, they all are part of the fiesta family.

But that's just this author's perception of Latin style. What's yours?

It all comes down to personality types, upbringing, and personal preferences. These are the elements that shape how each person will incorporate the designs into their sacred dwelling. To the elderly *nana,* it isn't about style at all. The religious shrine trimmed with Christmas tree lights, family photos, and prayer cards is all about heritage, respect, and faith. For the trendy teen in Spanish class, however, Latin style is pair of sterling-silver Mexican earrings purchased at an outdoor Tijuana market. At another point in the spectrum, it's a *macho cerveza*-friendly bar lined with Spanish bullfighter posters and vintage *serapes.* These are random examples that show how we all know someone who is enamored by the culture in one way or another.

Mestizo: Combining Cultures and Techniques

The word *mestizo* is all about blending ideas and inspirations. Technically, the term dates back to the sixteenth century when the Spaniards invaded Mexico, resulting in a new race of people. In the past the word had a negative connotation. But in recent times, *mestizo* has become quite the opposite. Its current meaning—the melting pot of people from all heritages—is something we all can relate to. And it doesn't only apply to bloodlines. Emerging from the *mestizo* movement is a whole new breed of Spanish-influenced artwork, which includes everything from tilework to the architecture of Spanish missions. The Mexican people haven't only expanded these concepts, they've also revitalized them by adding their own recipes of color, application, and flair.

When decorating your own *casa loca*, don't hesitate to take the daring *mestizo* approach. Join concepts, regions, and cultures, as well as techniques. *La Casa Loca* is all about celebrating diversity through an artistically wild conga line that dances to a different rhythm.

Mexican Pop Art

Latin style isn't only about tossing the serape on top of the couch. It also thrives on originality—converting the serape into fringed throw pillows and *then* tossing them on the couch. Welcome to the campy world that is known as pop art. It stems from turning everyday objects that are commonly taken for granted into lively accessories. Considered a tongue-in-cheek method of making fun, functional art out of ordinary objects, its subjects range from historical icons to children's games to religious saints to food containers. Some of the most beloved subjects used in Latin pop art are the legendary Mexican painters Frida Kahlo and Diego Rivera, the comical *Lucha Libre* wrestlers, *Dia de los Muertos* skeletons, and the sacred image of the Virgin of Guadalupe. These tangible topics are respectfully reinvented for the sake of decor—handbags, bottle cap crucifixes, picture frames, and furniture. Even if your only experience with Latin culture is watching Ricky Ricardo in an *I Love Lucy* rerun, there are plenty of ways to bring the wonderful genre of Latin style into your home and life. You won't be the first to try it, nor will you be the last.

Materials and Techniques

Just because your colorful ideas are doing some fancy mambo steps doesn't mean your organizational skills can join in. La casa loca may be happy, but la workspace loca can cause a crafting hangover. Consider this chapter the outlined diagram to the Creativity Cha-Cha.

We've all drooled over a Latin pop art piece and then raced home to duplicate it. However, it's easier said than done. It's likely that the materials the artist used are only found within his or her specific region or — gasp! — that the artist created them by hand. Don't get discouraged. Just loosen up and let your own ideas emerge. (Maybe a margarita will help. . .)

Getting Started

Begin by collecting an array of Latin-themed items to use in your projects: postcards, food labels, postage stamps, fabric scraps, stickers, bottle caps, phone cards, magazines, and small toys. These can be found at swap meets, grocery stores, thrift boutiques, and museum stores. If all else fails, plug in, sign on, and surf your way to online auctions and search engines.

Tips and Tricks

Clear an area roomy enough to allow for bursts of creativity and easy assembly.

Use plastic segmented trays or plastic sandwich bags to store small items.

Always sketch out designs before applying them to your final work.

For heavy objects that need to set quickly, add a dollop of industrial-strength glue to the center of the area, and then surround the edges with hot glue. This technique will hold the item in place until the industrial glue cures.

Make color copies of photos that you don't want to permanently attach to your work.

Add a protective sheen to images by brushing on a thin layer of white glue. Let it dry, and then varnish as usual. Do not varnish without sealing the image first, or it will seep though and ruin the picture.

Be safe. Always use gloves, a mask, and goggles for jobs that entail sharp tools or airborne fumes.

These art pieces are supposed to induce smiles. Keep up the momentum by grooving to Latin tunes while you work. Don't understand Spanish? Who cares? It's the rhythm and spirit of the music that are inspiring. Ozomatli, Los Tigres del Norte, Gilberto Santa Rosa, Manu Chao, and Shakira will do the trick.

Basic Materials

- Ψ You will need some supplies that can be purchased at craft, fabric, or home improvement stores. Here's a general rundown, but keep in mind, a materials list is a lot like an afternoon fiesta—the more the merrier.
- Ψ Scissors—basic and decorative edged
- Ψ Adhesives—white glue, glue sticks, a hot glue gun, industrial-strength glue
- Ψ Tapes—clear, double sided, and masking
- Ψ Measuring tape and ruler
- Ψ Hand drill, hammer, screws, and small nails
- Ψ Craft knife with assorted blades
- Ψ Paints—satin-finish sprays, water-based acrylics, and stained-glass gels
- Ψ Base coat and liner craft brushes
- Ψ Varnishes—high-gloss and matte spray, water-based brush-on polyurethane
- Ψ Colored pencils, paint pens, and wood stain markers
- Ψ Papers in different textures and designs
- Ψ Odds and ends—fishing line, jump rings, head pins, wire, needle-nosed pliers, tweezers, and clay-, tin-, or woodworking tools
- Ψ Fabrics, trims, stamps, and stencils
- Ψ Found objects and accessories—rhinestones, tassels, plastic flowers, small toys, coins, seashells, trinkets, glass, mirrors, wood cutouts, marbles, rocks, Mardi Gras beads, and raffia.

Home Accessories

Sometimes the best things come in small packages. Decorating with a Latin twist is no exception. When it comes to embellishing walls, furnishings, tabletops, or even whole rooms, those small packages translate into clever and cultural accent pieces.

The ideas in this chapter are simply eye candy exclamation points. They are meant to add brief splashes of festive cheer to ordinary areas that would benefit from a bit of perking up. Let your personality be your guide when determining how far you want to carry the Mexican theme. *¿Un pequeño o mucho?* (A little or a lot?) The projects in this chapter range from dainty ornaments and petite light-switch covers to wild wall shrines and vibrant sofa pillows. It's totally up to you to incorporate one design into your dwelling—or maybe more than a few.

Don't panic if these ideas seem a bit overwhelming at first. The beauty is that each art piece can be altered and adapted in color, shape, or theme to fit your home's decor. If primary acrylic *colores* (colors) are brighter than you prefer, soften them with a dash of white. Not into glitter? Colored sand adds the same dimensional effect without all that sparkly glitz. The impact of dangling trims and fringe can be taken down a notch by using them sparingly or not at all. Ultimately, each of these home accessory creations is ripe for fine-tuning for living rooms, family rooms, bedrooms, and even bathrooms. (Yes, it has been done before!) And when in doubt, remember one thing: A little color never hurt anyone.

Nifty Nicho Postcard Shrine

The next best thing to visiting exotic locations is collecting postcards from them. A nicho (small wall box) is a great way to incorporate your travel memories into an artful showpiece. In this example, the lid of a shallow cigar box has been altered to serve as a door that opens to display a vintage Mexican postcard. Trimmed in glitter and gold, the box is further embellished with miniature mirrors, stamps, and gems.

Materials

- ψ Cigar box with attached lid
- ψ Postcard
- ψ Acrylic paints in desired colors
- ψ Colored cardstock
- ψ Wooden ball ½" (3 cm) diameter
- ψ Accent pieces: Mardi Gras beads, copper wire, miniature mirrors, foil decorations
- ψ Loose glitter
- ψ Glass pebbles
- ψ Hot glue gun
- ψ Scissors
- ψ Craft knife
- ψ Saw-toothed picture hanger
- ψ Wood ball ½" (3 cm) diameter
- ψ Ruler
- ψ Pencil
- ψ Sandpaper

Makes one *nicho*

1. With a ruler and pencil, lightly draw a 4" × 4½" (10 cm × 11.5 cm) box in the center of the lid. Use a craft knife to remove the box to create a window in the lid. Sand the edges smooth.

2. Carefully remove the paper lining from the inside of the box, and then paint a basecoat in a desired color. Paint the inner sides of the box, and then sprinkle on the loose glitter. Use hot glue to add accents. With hot glue, trim the front window with Mardi Gras beads, and add the wooden ball as a knob.

3. Decorate the inner lid and top of the box.

4. Attach the postcard to colored cardstock, and apply the glass pebbles to the back with hot glue. Center the cardstock inside the box, and adhere. Add embellishments around the postcard's edges.

5. Attach a saw-toothed picture hanger on the back.

TIP Let each step dry before moving on to the next one. Use decorative-edged scissors to trim postcard. Add other personal mementos, such as coins, postage stamps, or letters.

Artist: Kathy Cano-Murillo
Dimensions: 8" × 12" (20.3 cm × 30.5 cm)

Fruit Crate Revolutionary Frame

This rustic frame is empowering on many levels. It was inspired by General Zapata (1879–1919) and the Mexican Revolution, as well as by the modern Zapatista movement in Chiapas and the south of Mexico. The original Zapatistas, who fought in the Mexican Revolution from 1910 to 1917, used the image of the Virgin of Guadalupe as their badge of identification as members of the peasant army. The style of the concha (a seashell motif, which is an ancient symbol of Christianity) at the top of the frame is reminiscent of traditional retablos, inlayed boxes that house hand-painted images of saints. Even more impressive is the fact that this beautiful piece originates from recycled rejas (grills), also know as the slats from Mexican fruit crates.

Materials

- Print or postcard image of Emiliano Zapata, 5" x 3" (12.5 cm x 7.5 cm)
- Basswood
- *Rejas* (slats from wooden fruit crates)
- Virgin of Guadalupe medal
- Template on page 118
- Acrylic paint
- White craft glue
- Twine and eye hooks
- Rusting agent
- Spray matte varnish
- Hammer and small nails
- White wood glue
- Scroll saw
- Decoupage medium
- Sponge brush
- Sandpaper

Makes one frame

1. Cut a piece of basswood measuring 5" × 3" (12.5 cm x 7.5 cm). Decoupage the print of Zapata onto it, let dry, and set aside.

2. Assemble the back of the frame by gluing two *rejas* together with two cross pieces, using white glue and small nails.

3. Trace the template on page 118 onto the basswood to create the scalloped trim for the top of the frame. Cut it out with scroll saw. To create the frame, split the *rejas* down the middle, and cut them to 5" (12.5 cm) long. Attach the pieces together with wood glue or small nails to create a flat rectangle.

4. Nail the frame pieces and the *concha* (scalloped trim) in place to the back piece of wood. Apply wood glue to all adjoining surfaces before you nail them together. Use as few nails as possible so they don't get in the way of the design. Paint the frame with watered-down acrylic paint to create a stained appearance.

5. Apply the rusting agent to the medal to age it, and then nail it to the top of the *concha*. Glue the image of Zapata to the center of the frame. Hold it firmly until it sets. Sand the edges to give the frame a rough look. Attach a piece of twine with eye hooks for hanging.

VARIATIONS You can use other types of wood measuring ¼" to ⅜" (.6 cm to 1 cm) in thickness in place of the *rejas.* You can use foam board in place of basswood if you do not have access to a scroll saw. To keep the picture protected, seal it with a spray matte varnish. For more detail, create three more *conchas* and attach them around the border of the frame.

Artist: Bryant "Eduardo" Holman
Dimensions: 9½" × 6" (24 cm × 15 cm)

Tree of Life Light-Switch Cover

Mexican clay renditions of Adam and Eve and the Tree of Life are seen in a variety of forms and functions, from elaborate candlesticks to tabletop sculptures and colorful wall hangings. Now you can create your own miniature version that will be just as impressive as the real thing. These vibrant and three-dimensional light-switch covers work for just about any situation. For rooms that are completely decorated, they add that last-needed bit of color. At the other end of the spectrum, this cover is the ultimate push to get that design overhaul of bare and bland rooms underway — not to mention that having the light on is great place to start.

Materials

- Ψ 1 blank light-switch cover
- Ψ White Sculpey brand clay
- Ψ Green, black, blue, yellow, red, gold-tone and flesh-colored acrylic paints
- Ψ Squeeze glitter in green, red, and multicolor
- Ψ Industrial-strength craft glue
- Ψ Water-based brush-on polyurethane varnish
- Ψ Assorted brushes
- Ψ Craft knife

Makes one light-switch cover

1. Working on a clean, flat surface, pinch off a chunk of clay and work it into a thin rectangle. Use the craft knife to cut out five braches from the top and five tree roots at the bottom. Attach the tree to the cover, and cut out the holes for the light switch and screws. Use your fingers to form the clay to the shape of the cover.

2. Create one body at a time from the clay by cutting out one thin 2" (5 cm) rectangle for the body, two small ½" × ⅛" (13 mm x 3 mm) rectangles for the arms, and a ¼" (6 mm) circle for the head. Arrange these pieces on either side of the tree. Pinch the clay to create the feet. Roll out a piece of clay for the snake, and lay it at the base of the tree. Create the fruit by making eight ⅛" (3 mm) balls of clay. Roll out a thin layer of the clay, and cut small leaves. Use the craft knife to make veins in the leaves, if desired. Apply the fruit and leaves to the cover.

3. Put the entire cover on a cookie sheet, and bake it in the oven at 150°F (65.5°C) for 30 to 40 minutes until the clay sets. Remove and let cool.

4. Carefully remove the pieces from the cover, and reapply them with the industrial-strength craft glue. Let dry, and then use the acrylic paint to color the background, leaves, snake, fruit, and people. Use the liner brush and black paint to create accents, followed by squeeze glitter on leaves and fruit. After everything is completely dry, brush on the water-based varnish to seal the cover.

VARIATION Create other themes for the cover by making roses and vines or a *Dia de los Muertos* scene.

Artist: Patrick Murillo
Dimensions: 5" × 3"
(12.5 cm × 7.5 cm)

Zoot Suit Night-Light

They were called pachucos. Flash back to the 1940s, and these zoot-suited rebels were all the rage of the dance halls and parties. Some call them the punk rockers of the Mexican-American communities that launched a fashion revolution still prevalent today. These young men expressed themselves through a flamboyant style that consisted of slicked-back ducktails, oversized pinstripe suits, wide-brimmed hats, two-toned shoes, and pocket watches that hung by a cadena (chain) from their belt loop, below their knee, and back up into their pocket. But none of those accessories were as crucial as the gorgeous girls by their side and a meticulously decorated set of wheels to cruise in.

Materials

- ψ 4 strips of basswood, 3½" x ½" (9 cm x 1.3 cm)
- ψ 1 strip of basswood, 2½" x ½" (6.5 cm x 1.3 cm)
- ψ 1 night-light, 3" (7.5 cm) long, with bulb
- ψ 1 piece of patterned vellum paper 3½" x 3½" (9 cm x 9 cm)
- ψ 4 strips of ribbon, 3½" x ½" (9 cm x 1.3 cm)
- ψ Template on page 119
- ψ Acrylic paint
- ψ Water-based brush-on polyurethane varnish
- ψ Assorted markers
- ψ Hot glue gun
- ψ Paintbrushes

Makes one night-light

1. Glue together the four strips of basswood to create a square frame. Paint a basecoat in a desired color.

2. Place the vellum paper on top of the template on page 119, and trace the design with a black marker. Color the design on the vellum paper with the colored markers, and adhere it to the frame using a hot glue gun. Trim with pieces of ribbon.

3. Paint the base of the night-light, let it dry, and then brush on a coat of varnish. Use hot glue to attach the small basswood strip to the front side of the casing of the bulb.

4. Run a bead of hot glue on the front of the small strip, and press the back of the frame to it. Hold together tightly with your fingers until it sets in place. Add a dab of glue to the adjoining sides.

Plug in and enjoy!

TIP Use only permanent markers to prevent smudging.

VARIATIONS Clear vellum paper, thin glass, or Plexiglas can be used in place of patterned vellum paper. Alternate the lengths of the wooden strips to make a larger light.

Artist: Kathy Cano-Murillo
Dimensions: 3½″ × 4½″ (9 cm × 11.5 cm)

Foaming Flan Soap Bars

It isn't often that an art project comes out good enough to eat, but we all know that looks are deceiving. Sink your teeth into this, and your mouth will bubble over with foam and lather. We're talking soap. Here we have a round bar that is created to look like the popular Mexican and Spanish dessert called flan. Considered the Latin form of crème brûlée, it is a type of creamy custard made from eggs and then baked in caramel sauce. Our flan ingredient list is short and sweet: melt-and-pour soap and food coloring. You can't eat it, but you can use it to wash your hands after devouring the real thing.

Materials

- Ψ Clear melt-and-pour soap base
- Ψ White melt-and-pour soap base
- Ψ Round plastic container or soap mold (preferably one that is flan shaped)
- Ψ 2 small glass dishes
- Ψ Brown food coloring
- Ψ Rubbing alcohol in spritz bottle
- Ψ Butcher's paper or paper towels
- Ψ Knife
- Ψ Microwave oven
- Ψ Plastic spoon or chopsticks

Makes one bar of soap

1. Line your work area with butcher's paper or paper towels. Cut 2 ounces (57 gm) from the clear and white soaps into 1" (2.5 cm) squares. Put the clear cubes in one glass dish and the white cubes in the other ones.

2. Beginning with the clear soap, microwave on high for 30-second intervals until liquefies. Add 3 or 4 drops of brown food coloring, and stir with a plastic spoon or chopsticks until the liquid reaches a caramel color. Pour a ⅜" (1 cm) layer of soap into the round soap mold, and let it cool thoroughly. Spritz with rubbing alcohol.

3. Repeat the melting process for the white soap. Add 2 drops of brown food coloring to it, and stir until blended to a tan consistency. Pour a ⅝" (1.5 cm) layer of soap on top of the clear brown soap in the mold. Allow the soap to cool.

4. Remove soap bar from mold.

5. Heat up leftover clear brown soap mixture. Let cool until a thick skin forms on top. Slowly pour over the top of the flan soap bar so that it dribbles down the sides. Let cool. Display on a doily and enjoy!

TIPS Use extreme caution because heated soap is very hot. If storing for later use or giving as gifts, wrap soaps in cellophane or in clear plastic bags with twist ties.

VARIATIONS Make sugar skull soap bars by pouring white melt-and-pour soap base into sugar skull molds and decorating with paint and sealing with a clear varnish. You can make lathering *loteria* soap bars as well. Pour a layer of melt-and-pour soap base in the mold, lay a laminated card face down, and then add another layer of soap.

Artist: Kerith Henderson
Dimensions: 1" × 3" (2.5 cm × 7.5 cm)

Fancy Fabric Wall Hanging

To stitch or not to stitch? That is the needling question for many creative minds that are intimidated by sewing machines. Fabric collage is one way to gently put your foot on the pedal and reap the rewarding results. There are no strict patterns or special cuts. The concept is to gather a variety of scraps in different patterns and textures and unify them into a free-flowing and festive wall hanging. Crooked corners, frayed edges, and contrasting colors are what make this work. With rules like that, a stitch in time sounds just fine.

Materials

- ψ 1 piece of fabric 24" x 12" (61 cm x 30.5 cm)

- ψ 1/5" (2.5 cm)-diameter dowel, 12" (30.5 cm) long

- ψ One 20" (51 cm) piece of ribbon for hanging

- ψ Fabric scraps and trim

- ψ Fabric piece to be used as the center focal point

- ψ Thread in assorted colors

- ψ Fabric roses

- ψ 12" (20.5 cm) strip of colored fringe

- ψ Hot glue gun

- ψ Hole punch

- ψ Sewing machine

Makes one fabric wall hanging

1. Lay the large piece of fabric on a flat surface. Sort your fabric scraps according to size, shape, or color. Choose one to be the focal point. Arrange a layout with all of the scraps on the fabric until you find a design you like.

2. Sew the centerpiece to the larger piece of fabric, leaving an extended border. Use the hot glue gun to attach the entire piece to the main piece of fabric, and follow up by sewing the pieces together.

3. Add different types of trim around the centerpiece, using contrasting colors of thread to add highlights. Sew the row of fringe along the bottom, and attach fabric roses in the corners.

4. Fold the top of the fabric collage over 1" (2.5 cm), and sew. Slide the dowel through. Punch two holes at the top directly under the dowel, thread the ribbon through, and gather at the top. Tie off and hang.

TIPS Decide ahead of time if you would like frayed edges and wrinkled fabric or hemmed edges and ironed fabric. Experiment with different types of ribbons and scraps before gluing the pieces in place.

VARIATIONS Skip step four if you would like to frame your piece under glass.
This project can be created as a "no-sew" project by using glue sticks and hot glue.
Transfer photos onto fabric to use as the centerpiece with the help of a computer
printer. Hem the sides of the fabric wall hanging with fabric adhesive, if desired.

Artist: Kathy Cano-Murillo
Dimensions: 30" × 12" (76 cm x 30.5 cm)

Reverse-Painted Box

From stained to sculptured, glass art is presented in all sorts of styles and methods. Somewhere in between is the process of reverse glass painting. Although originally from China, it is now known as one of the main art forms from Cajamarca, Peru. Each panel serves as a miniature masterpiece that features an intricate hand-painted image. It's also a technique that can be easily adapted for everyday crafts. Consider this multicolored box project to be Reverse Glass Painting 101.

Materials

Makes one box

- Ψ 4 pieces of glass, 3½" x 5" (9 cm x 12.5 cm)

- Ψ 4 pieces of balsa wood, 3½" x 5" each (9 cm x 12.5 cm)

- Ψ 1 square piece of thin wood, 3½" x 3½" (9 cm x 9 cm)

- Ψ Templates on page 120

- Ψ 4 wooden balls, ⅜" (1 cm) in diameter

- Ψ Acrylic paints

- Ψ Water-based brush-on polyurethane varnish

- Ψ Hot glue gun

- Ψ Industrial-strength glue

- Ψ 1 roll of foil tape, ½" (1.3 cm) wide

- Ψ Liner brush

- Ψ Window cleaner and paper towels

- Ψ Scissors

1. Clean each piece of glass with window cleaner and paper towel. Carefully trim each glass piece in foil tape to cover any sharp edges. Work with one piece of glass at a time on a flat surface. Place each template on the work surface, and then place the glass piece on top of the template.

2. Outline the design with the liner brush and black paint. Fill in the design with paint, and let dry. Coat with a water-based varnish. Attach each panel to a piece of balsa wood, and then apply another layer of foil tape to the edges to join the two pieces together. Paint the inner panels in a desired color.

3. Alternate using the hot glue and industrial-strength craft glue in 1" (2.5 cm) intervals to adjoin two of the panels. Connect the other panels in the same fashion. Let dry, and then add a strip of foil tape to all of the inner and outer adjoining edges for extra holding strength.

4. Attach the square piece of thin wood to the bottom of the box using the same glue-and-foil method. Use the hot glue to attach painted wooden balls for the feet.

TIPS You can wear gloves when working with the glass for extra protection. Make sure that all glue is completely dry before adding the foil tape. Use the box for lightweight items, such as cotton balls, letters, rubber bands, or pencils.

VARIATIONS Use smaller pieces of glass to make miniature boxes. Rubber stamps or other line drawings on paper can be used instead of the templates. Gold foil tape is also available. Create coasters by using the foil tape to adhere the glass pieces to cork or wood.

Artist: Kathy Cano-Murillo
Dimensions: 6" x 4" (15 cm x 10 cm)

Stamped
Folk Art Boxes

In this project, rubber stamping reaches a whole new level—literally. These miniature boxes look as though they were painstaking hand-carved with intensive skill, precision, and labor. Actually, the process is quite simple. The secret is to apply Aztec-themed rubber stamps to pieces of air-dry clay and then accent the surface with color.

Materials

- 1 small chipwood or papier-mâché box
- DAS air-dry terra-cotta clay
- Small Aztec or other ethnic-themed rubber stamps
- Acrylic paints in two or three desired colors
- Gold-toned acrylic paint
- Water-based brush-on polyurethane varnish
- White glue
- Small craft brushes
- Clay roller
- Craft knife
- Paint brushes

Makes one box

1. Work on a clean, flat surface. Pinch off a chunk of clay, and use the roller to flatten it to a ¼" (6 mm) thickness. Cover the box with the clay, one side at a time, and trim it to size using the craft knife. Do not cover the area where the lid overlaps the box. Return the pieces to a flat surface.

2. Stamp each piece. Use the craft brush to paint a layer of white glue onto the surface of the box, and adhere each stamped piece one by one. Let the clay and glue dry for several hours.

3. Paint the uncovered areas of the box (such as inside the box, lip, and lid) in a desired color, and let dry.

4. Use your finger to gently rub one color of paint across the stamped clay. Repeat the process with an additional color, and once more with the gold-toned paint.

5. Varnish the box with a craft brush and water-based varnish. Let dry.

TIP Smooth out cracks in the clay or blend areas together by dipping your finger in water and gently rubbing the area.

VARIATION Use this process to decorate larger pieces of art, such as picture frames, jewelry boxes, or flowerpots.

Artist: Kathy Cano-Murillo
Dimensions: 3" x 3" x 1½" (7.5 cm x 7.5 cm x 4 cm)

Mirrored Mission Ornaments

With twinkling lights, glass bulbs, and sparkling trim, it's no wonder that holiday trees are so much fun. Add an array of handmade tin ornaments, and your tree will be the best on the block. The two key elements in this project are the embossing tin and the glass paint. By combining techniques and easy-to-use applications, a batch of these shiny hanging charms can be made in an afternoon. Don't forget to make an extra batch to give to friends and family or to hang from wrapped gifts. The beautiful Mexican mission churches of the Southwest inspired the pattern, which will also add a touch of enlightenment to the season. ¡ Feliz Navidad!

Materials

- Ψ 5" x 5" (12.5 cm x 12.5 cm) piece of embossing tin
- Ψ 2" x 2" (5 cm x 5 cm) mirror for each ornament
- Ψ Template on page 121
- Ψ Cardstock
- Ψ Squeezable glass paints
- Ψ Raffia
- Ψ Multicolored gems
- Ψ 1 sheet of white typing paper
- Ψ Hot glue gun
- Ψ Craft knife
- Ψ Hole punch
- Ψ Magazine
- Ψ Embossing tool
- Ψ Toothpick
- Ψ Scissors

Makes one ornament

1. Trace the template on page 121 onto a piece of white typing paper, and cut out the shape. Lay the cutout on top of the piece of embossing tin, and cut out the shape again. Repeat the process on a piece of cardstock, and set it aside for later use. Using the craft knife, carefully slice three lines in the center of the tin to create little "doors."

2. Lay the tin on a magazine, and use the embossing tool to draw designs on the face of the ornament and on the little doors. Flip the tin over. Apply a line of hot glue around the outer edge of the mirror, and place it face down in the center of the back of the tin.

3. Turn the ornament over again. Use a toothpick to apply glass paint to the embossed designs. When finished, let the paint dry completely. Add gems as accents, if desired.

4. Glue the cardstock to the back of the mission ornament, and trim any edges that overlap. Open the little doors so the mirror shows through. Punch a hole at the top and hang with raffia.

TIP The center of a cookie sheet and a sharp pencil can be used in place of the embossing tin and tool.

VARIATIONS Draw patterns of your own to make a variety of ornaments, such as hearts, diamonds, suns, or stars. Instead of making little doors, cut a circle or a square out of the center. The mirror can be replaced with a favorite picture.

Artist: Kathy Cano-Murillo
Dimensions: 4" x 3" (10 cm x 7.5 cm)

Peso Picture Frame

Avoiding Mexican mercados is as unheard of as ordering a basket of tortilla chips without the salsa. From Mexicali to Mazatlan, each city offers a treasure trove of treats to buy and bring home. Hats, toys, food, magazines, furniture, and more are all available for a price, thanks to the gracious vendors that are known for wheeling and dealing. It doesn't matter if the purchase is as grande as a luxurious leather sofa or as poco as a pack of peppermint chicle, loose change is always a factor. No matter what, there is always some left over. Make the most of it by using a handful of those spare Mexican pesos to add some cultural value to a picture frame. Unless, that is, you need them for your next "South of the Border" shopping trip.

Materials

- Ψ 8" x 10" (20.5 cm x 25.5 cm) piece of glass and backing
- Ψ 10" x 12" (25.5 cm x 30.5 cm) wood frame, with a 2" (5 cm)-wide border
- Ψ Acrylic paints in yellow, lime green, blue, and purple
- Ψ 28–30 assorted peso coins
- Ψ Industrial-strength glue
- Ψ Sandpaper
- Ψ Saw-toothed picture hanger or easel stand
- Ψ Paintbrush

Makes one frame

1. Lightly sand the frame, and then paint a basecoat of yellow. Let the paint dry, and then repeat the process with the remaining colors. Let each color dry between coats.

2. Sand the entire surface so that the layered colors show through. You should be able to see all the colors on the wood.

3. Working on a flat surface, set the frame down and arrange the coins around the border to create a balanced look. Working one coin at a time, add a small dollop of glue, and press the coin firmly to the frame's surface. Let it dry for several hours.

4. Insert the glass and backing. Add either the saw-toothed picture hanger or an easel stand.

TIPS Keep checking the coins as you glue them to make sure they don't slide out of place. Pesos can also be purchased at various financial institutions.

VARIATIONS Use more coins to create a random collage-like design, or add grout to make a mosaic.

Artist: Kathy Cano-Murillo
Dimensions: 10" x 12" (25.5 cm x 30.5 cm)

Gardening

A happy Mexican garden means a happy Mexican meal—if you're the type that grows your own veggies, that is. Whether you are planting jalapeño seeds for an upcoming salsa marathon or tending to a batch of elegant *nopales* (prickly pear cactus), don't neglect livening up your leafy landscapes. Plants are living entities that thrive in positive, fruitful surroundings, much like humans.

Isn't that reason enough to create original art pieces for the garden? Of course!

Red, green, and yellow jalapeños nestled inside a bowl look as zesty and spicy as they taste. Aside from inducing a craving for a cool glass of *sangria* (wine), the combo also conjures up images of gorgeous Mexican gardens that are bursting with brightly curved bell peppers, long ears of multicolored corn, and blooming *flores* (flowers). Keep this imagery in mind when accessorizing your flowerbeds and greenery with South of the Border flair.

Before getting too excited, take time to explore your garden or patio. If it makes you feel serene and peaceful, make a Mexican Cowgirl Wind Chime (page 46) to add gentle tunes to the air. Maybe it reflects whimsy and friendliness: The Mexicali Mini-Lights (page 54) work wonders for adding the right illumination to those inspiring conversations.

The idea is to carry the mood you want to develop into your work—and workspace. If you live in a climate that offers wonderful weather, set up an art table outdoors so you can make cultural creations within the environment in which you will display them.

Once you've outfitted the garden with all sorts of handmade *tesoros* (treasures), share the idea seeds! The projects in this chapter make for expressive, heartfelt gifts for favorite friends and loved ones. Think of it as snipping a branch from your imagination tree and passing it on for others to nurture in their own special way.

Tin Plant Pokes

The sad part about holiday decorations is the need to pack them up and send them to the storage room for the next 11 months. Just say no when it comes to doing this to Mexican tin ornaments. There are so many year-round ways to use the many happy shapes and themes that they come in: armadillos, cats, cacti, bulls, angels, hearts — the list goes on. For this project, they stay among the greenery, but not in their original use. After being glued to a shish kebob skewer, they become vibrant plant pokes. It's just a little reminder to keep the uplifting holiday cheer year-round.

Materials

ψ Mexican tin ornament

ψ Shish kebob skewer

ψ Water-based acrylic paints

ψ Industrial-strength craft glue

ψ Paintbrush

ψ Scissors

Makes one plant poke

1. Snip off the notch for hanging at the top of the ornament.

2. Place a 1" (2.5 cm) dollop of glue on the flat side of the shish kebab skewer, and press it to the back of the ornament. Set aside face-down until the glue is completely dry.

3. Paint the skewers to match the ornaments.

4. Insert the poke into the soil next to plants.

VARIATIONS Make an assortment of plant pokes by using different ornaments. Add strands of ribbon for more color.

Artist: Kathy Cano-Murillo
Dimensions: 12" x 4" (30.5 cm x 10 cm)

Aztec Cactus Garden

Let the Aztec gods grace your garden by way of this chunky cactus dish garden. Painted in bright and bold primary colors, its only purpose is to provide a fertile cultural home for all your favorite succulents, aloes, and agaves. Not into cacti? It also doubles as a candleholder, a fruit bowl, or even a zesty place for the basic potted plant.

Materials

- ᴪ 1 terra-cotta planter's pot, 8½" (21.5 cm)
- ᴪ 1 terra-cotta dish, 11" (28 cm)
- ᴪ Template on page 122
- ᴪ Assorted acrylic paints
- ᴪ Water-based brush-on polyurethane varnish
- ᴪ Industrial-strength craft glue
- ᴪ White craft glue
- ᴪ Paintbrushes

Makes one cactus garden

1. Paint a basecoat on the pot and the dish in contrasting colors. Paint detail patterns around the top rim of the saucer. Varnish and set aside.

2. Make four color copies of the Aztec picture template, and cut them out. Turn the pot upside down, and glue the copies around the pot with white craft glue. Dab your finger in the white glue, and rub a thin layer of glue over the entire surface of each of the four pictures.

3. Paint primitive patterns around the bottom and top of the pot and around the pictures. Let dry, and then varnish the pot.

4. Apply a generous amount of industrial-strength craft glue to the top of the upside-down pot. Set the dish on top of it, and move it around until it looks even from every angle.

5. Let dry for 24 hours before using.

TIP If you plan to transport this project, flip it over. Otherwise, it is top-heavy and easily breakable.

VARIATIONS Replace the Aztec pictures with other kinds of images.
Use rubber stamps in place of freehand detail painting.

Artist: Patrick Murillo
Dimensions: 13" x 12" (33 cm x 30.5 cm)

Glittery Soda Pop Vases

On a dry, hot day, there is nothing more refreshing than an icy cold soda. This project is the ultimate homage to the many tasty Mexican carbonated beverages on the market. But it's not just the distinctive drinks that are appealing; their bottles are also a treasure. They are usually embossed, painted, and decorated to match the theme of the bubbly contents. Glitter not only intensifies this art, but also celebrates it.

Materials

- Empty Mexican soda pop bottle
- Assorted colors of dry micro-glitter with applicator tip
- Acrylic paints
- High-gloss spray varnish
- Assorted brushes
- Toothpick
- Small dish

Makes one vase

1. Thoroughly wash and dry the bottle. Begin working from the inside of the design out. Squeeze the desired color of paint into a small dish. Dip the toothpick in the paint, and carefully trace over the letters on the label. Quickly sprinkle the dry micro-glitter over the paint so it sticks. Touch up any areas that were missed. Continue the process of finishing the entire label in different colors of micro-glitter. For larger areas, use a liner brush. Let dry.

2. Repeat the process for the top of the bottle.

3. Cover the remaining and largest area of the bottle with a larger brush, working a section at a time.

4. Let dry, and then look over the bottle for any bare spots. Fill in as needed.

5. Seal with a high-gloss spray varnish. Let dry, and then add your favorite flowers.

TIP Use bottles that have the label painted or embossed on them, as opposed to paper labels. Save the bottle caps to make the pins on page 98.

VARIATIONS This glitter-painting technique can be used on just about any surface. For a lighter look, use micro-glitter glue instead of paint.

Artist: Kathy Cano-Murillo
Dimensions: 9" x 2½" (23 cm x 6.5 cm)

Mexican Cowgirl Wind Chime

Mexican women have always been thought of as symbols of strength that tightly weave a family together with love, discipline, compassion, and a sense of humor. Enter the vaqueras — also known as the Mexican cowgirl — female ranchers who added a whole new level to that concept. These were bold and brave mujeres (women) who really knew how to hold down a hacienda. Whereas modern-day vaqueras still roam the ranches today, it was the vintage cowgirls who set the standard for roping, riding, and sometimes fighting in the old West. Perhaps the gentle sounds from this wind chime will summon and even harness a bit of that biting spirit from days gone by.

Materials

- ψ 2 unwanted CDs
- ψ 2 sheets of contrasting stationery paper
- ψ 2 pictures from Mexican cowgirl postcards
- ψ 3 chimes
- ψ 3 jump rings, ⅜" (1 cm)
- ψ 2 colors of crepe paper
- ψ String of beads
- ψ Loose glitter or squeeze glitter
- ψ Embroidery thread
- ψ 18-gauge wire
- ψ Hot glue gun
- ψ White craft glue
- ψ Hand drill
- ψ Scissors

Makes one wind chime

1. Trace the shape of the CD onto the two sheets of stationery paper. Cut out the circles so that you have one piece from each color of paper. Use the hot glue gun to attach a paper circle to one side of each CD.

2. Lay the CDs on a flat surface with the stationery paper side up. Cut out two cowgirl pictures, and affix one to the empty side of each CD. Trim the edges of the picture with glitter, and add painted designs, if desired.

3. Cut two strips of different colored crepe paper measuring 20" (51 cm) each. Attach them with hot glue to the back of each CD in a ruffled fashion. Repeat the process to attach the string of beads to front of each CD, creating a border to hide the edge of the CD. Drill a hole at the top of each CD and two holes at the bottom of one and one hole at the bottom of the other. Add a jump ring to each hole. Then use the hot glue to join the two CDs together.

4. Cut three strands of embroidery thread measuring 6" (15 cm) each. Thread one strand through each chime, and tie it to a jump ring hanging from the bottom of the CDs.

5. Cut a 6" (15 cm) piece of wire, and feed it through the holes at the top of the CDs. Bend to create a loop for hanging.

VARIATIONS Add another CD to create a longer chime.
Cut the CDs in half to create half-moon shapes.

Artist: Kathy Cano-Murillo
Dimensions: 12" x 4½" (30.5 cm x 11.5 cm)

Milagro Tree Ribbons

One of the most popular features in Mexican folk art is the milagro (miracle). In Mexican and Latin American culture, it is believed that carrying or offering one of these tiny charms will bring divine intervention to those who need it most. They are handmade in dozens of shapes, such as arms, hearts, legs, heads, animals, breasts, eyes, and many other specific styles. Those seeking guidance from a higher power present them to ofrendas (altars) as gifts or have them blessed and then pin them to undergarments for protection. Some are just kept in a special place in the home. However, we also see them used as an ethereal touch in contemporary artwork, including crosses, nichos, boxes, and jewelry pieces. This project puts their wondrous power to work as shimmering tree ornaments that are meant to bring a sense of happiness and inspiration to your home and garden setting.

Materials

- Ψ 1 piece of colored ribbon, 18" (45.5 cm) long
- Ψ 8 wooden disks, 1½" (4 cm) in diameter
- Ψ 8 *milagros*
- Ψ 14 miniature mirrors
- Ψ Crafting tin
- Ψ Acrylic paint in assorted colors
- Ψ Water-based brush-on polyurethane varnish
- Ψ Hot glue gun
- Ψ Scalloped-edged scissors
- Ψ Paintbrush

Makes one ribbon

1. Paint a basecoat on both sides of the disks in desired colors, and let dry. With the scalloped-edged scissors, cut four 2" (5 cm) circles from the tin. Glue a tin circle to each of the four wooden disks.

2. Lay the ribbon on a flat surface. Make a 2" (5 cm) loop for hanging at the top of the ribbon. Add hot glue to one wooden disk, and press it against the loop from the bottom up. Quickly press another wooden disk on the other side of the ribbon, creating a ribbon "sandwich." Continue this process with the miniature mirrors as well, alternating between mirrors and wooden disks. Allow the excess portion of the ribbon to hang down.

3. Glue a *milagro* to both sides of all wooden disks (eight in total). Coat with polyurethane for outside use.

VARIATION Fishing line can be used in place of ribbon and miniature tiles for mirrors.

Artist: Kathy Cano-Murillo
Dimensions: 18" x 2" (45.5 cm x 5 cm)

Spicy Candle Lanterns

Much like a shot of tequila, every digested jalapeño has a tale to tell. Whether inflicting a bout of "extreme watery eyes" syndrome or causing a grown man to scream out in pain, canned chilies sure can spice up mealtime. Don't toss the can just yet. Save it. Respect it. Know it. Keep a flame burning in it so it may forever serve as a reminder of what could be if its contents fall onto the wrong taste buds. You have been warned.

Materials

- Ψ One 8-ounce (227 gm) can of Mexican chilies
- Ψ 3 pieces of chain, 8" (20.5 cm) each
- Ψ Jump rings, 3/8" (1 cm)
- Ψ Dangling charm
- Ψ Glass votive holder
- Ψ Votive or tea light candle
- Ψ Hand drill
- Ψ Can opener
- Ψ Sandpaper

Makes one lantern

1. Remove the top of the can. Empty, thoroughly clean, and dry the can. Sand the edges at the ridge to remove any sharp points.

2. Drill three holes at the top of the can (just below the ridge) in a triangle fashion, in order to attach the chains. Drill two holes close together at the bottom of the can. Attach a jump ring to each hole at the top and one through the two holes at the bottom.

3. Hook one chain strip to each jump ring. Gather them at the top, and connect with two jump rings. Add a dangling charm to the bottom jump ring.

4. Insert the glass votive holder and candle into the can. Hang and light.

TIP Do not hang the lantern in direct sunlight, unless you want it to rust.

VARIATIONS Use another type of food can to add contrast. Instead of a basic chain, use a silver Guatemalan wedding necklace or coiled colored wire. Remove the label from a basic can, and paint your own designs on it.

Artist: Kathy Cano-Murillo
Dimensions: 16" x 3" (40.5 cm x 7.5 cm)

Cigar Box Birdhouse and Feeder

Not a fan of cigars? Don't let that stop you from partaking in the beautiful boxes that house pungent robustos. Luckily, purchasing the cigars isn't necessary for this project. Simply swing by the local smoke shop, and ask to purchase the empty sliding-door boxes. If the opportunity arises, pick up more than one. Let the different shapes and sizes appeal to you—and to the feathered friends that will soon appreciate a sweet-smelling home.

Materials

- Ψ Wooden cigar box with a sliding lid
- Ψ Charm (a "dangler")
- Ψ Colored ribbon, 6" (15 cm)
- Ψ 2 pieces of 24-gauge wire, 2" (5 cm) each
- Ψ Beads, clay pieces, colored rocks (for accents)
- Ψ Water-based brush-on polyurethane varnish
- Ψ Wood glue
- Ψ Industrial-strength craft glue
- Ψ Needle-nosed pliers
- Ψ Pencil
- Ψ Hot glue gun
- Ψ Hand drill or jigsaw

Makes one birdhouse

1. Draw a 2" (5 cm) circle on the lid of the box, and use the hand drill or a jigsaw to cut it out.

2. Drill two small holes on the top and bottom of the box. Thread wire through, and twist the ends inside the box using the needle-nosed pliers. Use the industrial-strength craft glue to adhere the ends permanently.

3. Run a thin bead of wood glue along the edge of the lid, and slide it into place.

4. Brush on a layer of water-based varnish. Let the box dry, and repeat the process.

5. Add decorative embellishments on the front and back of the birdhouse. Loop the piece of colored ribbon through the wire at the top. Add a dangling charm at the bottom.

TIP If using outside in direct sunlight, add several extra coats of varnish for protection.

VARIATIONS Instead of drilling a circle, glue the lid so that there is a partial opening at the bottom, and add birdseed to make it a feeder.

Artist: Kathy Cano-Murillo
Dimensions: 4½" x 6" x 4"
(11.5 cm x 15 cm x 10 cm)

Mexicali Mini-Lights

These days, you can find patio lights to match the wildest of themes. If pink flamingos, Barbie heads, or flying saucers don't light up your life, maybe these terra-cotta twinklers will. The combination of scrap ribbon, fabric, paint, glitter, and upside-down pots is all it takes to assemble awesome lights that are cool enough to rival any plastic manufactured set.

Materials

- Ψ String of 12 white miniature lights
- Ψ 12 miniature terra-cotta pots, 2" (5 cm) each
- Ψ 1 yard of solid-color ribbon
- Ψ 1 yard of multicolored ribbon
- Ψ 2 packages of embroidery thread
- Ψ White acrylic paint
- Ψ Water-based brush-on varnish
- Ψ Star glitter
- Ψ White craft glue
- Ψ Hot glue gun
- Ψ Paintbrushes
- Ψ Scissors

Makes one strand of lights

1. Turn all of the pots upside down. Paint six of them white on the main base, and trim the rims with the multicolored ribbon using the hot glue gun.

2. Leave the remaining six pots unpainted, but attach the solid-color ribbon around the rims with hot glue. Brush a thin layer of white craft glue on the main base of each of these six pots, and sprinkle the star glitter over it. Pat the star glitter in place with your fingertip.

3. Apply a coat of varnish to the bases and tops of all the pots.

4. Cover the light cord by wrapping the embroidery thread around it from one end to another. Add a dab of hot glue to seal the ends.

5. Use a blade from the scissors to widen the hole at the top of each pot so a light will fit through it snugly. Attach the plastic casing of the light to the pot with hot glue for extra hold. Hang, plug in, and light.

TIPS Make sure to hang the lights low enough so that you can easily replace the bulbs. Always use caution when working with electrical objects. Read the directions on the package for safety measures.

VARIATIONS Cover the pots entirely in fabric, or decoupage pictures on them. Add fringe around the rim instead of ribbon. Use a masonry bit to drill holes in the base of the pot for more light to shine through. Coordinate the lights to match your holiday decor, and hang them on a tree.

Artist: Kathy Cano-Murillo
Dimensions: 1 ½" x 2" (4 cm x 5 cm)

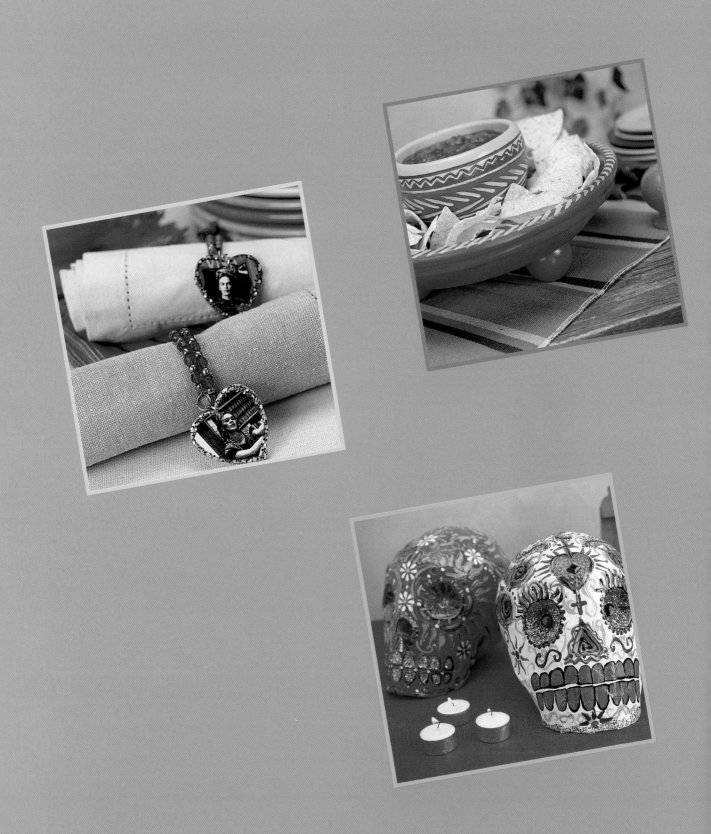

Fiesta

Recipe for a friendly fiesta:

1 part food • 1 part drink • 2 parts music

Instructions: Combine elements, add a dash of attitude, and mix with your favorite people. Garnish with killer party favors and decorations.

Now that you have the correct formula, it's time to put it to use. Although the next few pages can't fulfill every aspect mentioned, they will lend assistance to most. This chapter delves into the grand *piñata* that is party presentation.

What's the use of slaving over a hot stove all day if the table setting falls as flat as a deflated *sopaipilla* (turnover)? Don't your enchanting enchiladas deserve better? Of course! By all means, check out the wild and flaming *Dia de los Muertos* Serving Tray on page 66 for inspiration.

The art designs also extend beyond the edible. Therefore, you'll have to take that napkin from your lap and set it on the table—the craft table that is. You'll need it to wipe up any messy paint or glue spills that come from whipping up a batch of salt-rimmed margarita candles, or maybe assembling some funny Mexican wrestler place-card holders. For an elegant touch, learn how to wrap gift boxes to resemble a romantic Spanish balcony.

Impressed? Wait until you see the delighted faces on your party guests when they arrive. It's then you'll realize that all the hard work was worth it, hot stove and all. Just keep one thing in mind—the key ingredient that pulls it all together is undiluted imagination.

And we all know you have plenty of that.

Frida Kahlo Fiesta Placemats

It wasn't until after Frida Kahlo's death in 1954, that her art became appreciated worldwide — so much so, in fact, that she became an icon of Mexican culture. To this day, women of all ages and races adore this passionate and pained artist who was just as talented in the kitchen as she was in her studio. These placemats pay homage to Frida and her flavorful recipes. Even if you can't tell a tortilla from a tamale, you can still have a bit of her energy and spirit at mealtime.

Materials

- Ψ 1 sheet of colored paper, 18" x 13" (45.5 cm x 33 cm)
- Ψ Assorted images of Frida Kahlo
- Ψ Laminate sheet
- Ψ Ribbon, raffia
- Ψ Crepe paper
- Ψ Glue stick
- Ψ Scissors
- Ψ Hole punch
- Ψ Hot glue gun

Makes one placemat

1. Arrange your images in an appealing fashion on the colored paper. Use large pictures as the focal points, and add smaller items around them. Once you find a layout you are happy with, glue everything down with the glue stick.

2. Use the hot glue gun to add a trim of ribbon around the border of the paper, as well as an extended border of crepe paper.

3. At your local copy center, make a color copy of your finished design and have it laminated. Trim any excess, leaving a 1½" (4 cm) border. Store your original design in a safe place.

4. Punch holes along the short sides of the placemat, and tie raffia tassels from each one.

TIP Make a set of placemats by making and laminating more color copies. By storing the original, you can make new placemats as needed.

VARIATION To make a smaller placemat or coaster set, use smaller paper or reduce the image on the copy machine.

Artist: Kathy Cano-Murillo
Dimensions: 20" × 16"
(51 cm × 40.5 cm)

Flowered Balcony Gift Tower

Gift wrapping has just crossed the threshold of a whole new dimension. The grand haciendas of Mexico, as well as the coastal villas in Spain, inspired this ornate, lush gift tower. It's at places like these that the tiered balconies are overflowing with beautiful fresh flowers and hand-painted pottery. The concept works perfectly as a housewarming gift, with one gift assigned to each box: towels, candles, chocolates, oven mitts, placemats, small books, and more. However, the receiver shouldn't be heartbroken about dismantling the masterpiece. After the presents are removed, it can be easily reassembled and used as part of a home's decor.

Materials

- Ψ 5 round craft paper boxes, in graduated sizes with lids
- Ψ 4 yards (3.7 m) of olive green silk-look fabric, for bow treatments around each box edge
- Ψ 7 miniature terra-cotta pots, 2" (5 cm)
- Ψ 2 miniature wall pots (flat on one side) with foam inserts
- Ψ 4 yards (3.7 m) of Southwest-style ribbon for trimming the edges of the box lids
- Ψ 2 yards (1.8 m) of ribbon to cascade down the sides of the box tower
- Ψ ½ yard (46 cm) of miniature ribbon for the terra-cotta pots
- Ψ 16 miniature silk flower bunches for pots and trim
- Ψ 1 sheet of rub-off transfer flowers for miniature wall pots
- Ψ 7 faux sugar-dipped pears for the miniature pots and one for the top
- Ψ Double-stick foam tape
- Ψ Tape measure
- Ψ Hot glue gun
- Ψ Glue

Makes one gift tower

1. Place gift items inside of each box. Wrap and glue the trim on the edges of the box lids.

2. Measure the fabric around each box base. Spot-glue the fabric around the edges to hold it in place. Tie bows in front of each box, and secure with hot glue. Do not put a bow on the top box—just wrap the edge with ribbon.

3. Once each box is completed, stack all but the top box in a graduated order. Secure the boxes to each other with double-stick foam tape. Glue one faux sugar-dipped pear into each miniature terra-cotta pot, and attach the miniature ribbon to the sides of the pots with the hot glue. Arrange the pots around the top edge of box three, and secure them in place with hot glue.

4. Transfer the rub-off flowers onto the sides of the miniature wall pots, and arrange the flowers inside of them. Glue the pots to the sides of box three. Scatter a few of the silk flowers around the bases of the wall pots, and glue them in place.

5. Using a tape measure, determine the length from the base to the top of the tower, and then add 3" (7.5 cm). Cut four lengths of ribbon matching the final measurement. These four ribbons will cascade down the sides of the entire stack of boxes. Glue the four ribbons on top of box two. They will fall down the sides of the stack of boxes. Use the hot glue to attach the ends of the ribbons to the underside of the large box at the bottom of the stack.

6. Attach the smallest box to the top of the stack using the double-stick foam tape. Secure the last miniature terra-cotta pot with the pear to the top of the box with the hot glue.

VARIATION For a less complex project, use only one or two boxes.

Artist: Michelle Zecchini Cano
Dimensions: 24" × 14" (61 cm × 35.5 cm)

Hot, Hot, Hot! Chips and Salsa Set

A fiesta without chips and salsa is like a piñata without candy. Never underestimate the conversational power of warm and crispy corn chips accompanied by juicy, salty, and searing salsa. Honor this timeless tradition by delivering the spicy goods with mucho flavor and character. This ordinary terra-cotta saucer and planter set goes above and beyond its normal course of garden duty to become a dazzling centerpiece that screams hot, hot, hot!

Materials

ψ 1 terra-cotta saucer 12" (30.5 cm)

ψ 1 round planter 3" x 5" (7.5 cm x 12.5 cm)

ψ 1 glass bowl to fit inside the planter

ψ 3 round balls, 2" (5 cm) in diameter

ψ 3 glass pebbles

ψ Assorted acrylic paints

ψ Water-based brush-on polyurethane varnish

ψ Craft brushes

ψ Industrial-strength craft glue

ψ Paintbrushes

Makes one chips and salsa set

1. Paint the entire surface of the saucer, planter, and balls with the acrylic paint. Add detailed designs, as desired.

2. Use industrial-strength craft glue to adhere the balls in a triangle pattern to the bottom of the saucer and the glass pebbles to the bottom of the planter.

3. Use a craft brush to apply several layers of water-based varnish to the planter and saucer. Let dry in between coats, and wait 24 hours before using. Insert glass bowl into the planter.

TIPS To clean after using, gently wipe the surface with a damp cloth. Occasionally revarnish the planter and saucer to keep them looking new.

VARIATIONS Use other types of planters for the middle. Use smaller sets for smaller tables.

Artist: Kathy Cano-Murillo
Dimensions: 12" × 6" (30.5 cm × 15 cm)

Tissue Flower Topiary

What's a party without breathtaking decorations? Even if the menu, games, party favors, and music are festive, the party isn't a success until the guests arm-wrestle over who gets to keep the table centerpiece. Keep that competitive spirit alive by whipping up a vivid, multicolored tissue-flower topiary for your next social gathering. With a bit of time, finger twirling, and scissor snipping, ordinary, inexpensive rolls of party streamers are transformed into lush miniature paper flowers. When combined, they make for a bright and cheery statement that is sure to liven up any fiesta.

Materials

- Ψ 1 floral Styrofoam topiary, 12" (30.5 cm)
- Ψ 6" (15 cm) terra-cotta pot and matching saucer
- Ψ 2 packages of 3" (7.5 cm) green-wired wooden floral picks (180 total)
- Ψ 8 rolls of crepe paper party streamers (red, yellow, orange, green, blue, purple, fuchsia)
- Ψ 1 bunch of faux greenery
- Ψ Acrylic paints
- Ψ Water-based brush-on polyurethane varnish
- Ψ Hot glue gun
- Ψ Scissors

TIPS Use decorative-edged scissors to trim the edges of your flowers to add dimension. Use single-color flowers to conserve the crepe paper.

Makes one topiary

1. Cut approximately 20 6" (15 cm) strips of each color of crepe paper. Take two strips of contrasting colors, and line them up together. Beginning with one end, roll the paper around the top of a wired wooden pick, while pinching the bottom of it as you go around the stick. When you reach the end of the paper, wrap the wire tightly around the bottom of the paper to secure it. Continue the process to make approximately 100 flowers.

2. Turn the Styrofoam topiary upside down, and insert a row of flowers at the underside of the ball, spacing them approximately ¾" (2 cm) apart. Fluff each flower as you go. Continue until either the entire ball is covered or you run out of flowers. Make more flowers, if necessary, to fill in any empty spots. Attach some faux greenery at random spots with the hot glue until you achieve a balanced look.

3. Wrap the stem of the topiary with two layers of green crepe paper, securing it with hot glue. Accent the stem with faux greenery. Decorate the base of the topiary in the same fashion, adding a layer of greenery that extends beyond the edge.

4. Paint the terra-cotta pot and saucer in desired colors, and let dry. Varnish if desired.

5. Insert topiary into terra-cotta pot.

VARIATION These flowers can be made without using the wired wooden picks. Simply roll the crepe paper into the flower shape, and tie it off with thin wire. Attach them to string to make a decorative garland.

Artist: Kathy Cano-Murillo
Dimensions: 24" × 8" (61 cm × 20.5 cm)

Día de los Muertos Serving Tray

An angel on one shoulder and a devil on the other — we've all been there. It's always at social gatherings when this odd couple emerges to spin your mind between choosing nice or naughty. No problem here, though. This fantastically far-out tray sports a dubious devil whose only intention is to induce good, clean fun. He is simply the clownish centerpiece on a painted disk that can carry an array of delicious, tempting finger foods. Go ahead, indulge. There are worse things you could do.

Materials

- Ψ 12" (30.5 cm) circular piece of wood
- Ψ Photocopy of a *Día de los muertos* image
- Ψ 13" (33 cm) of rope, ¼" (6 mm) in diameter
- Ψ 1 piece of flashing, 18" x 18" (45.5 cm x 45.5 cm)
- Ψ Acrylic paints
- Ψ Water-based brush-on polyurethane varnish
- Ψ Decoupage medium
- Ψ Felt
- Ψ Hot glue gun and industrial-strength craft glue
- Ψ Paintbrushes
- Ψ Heavy-duty scissors or tin snips
- Ψ Small nails and hammer
- Ψ Piece of paper and pencil

Makes one serving tray

1. Attach the rope around the perimeter of the wooden circle with the hot glue. Add 4 to 6 nails to secure it in place. Apply a basecoat of black acrylic paint on the wood and the rope.

2. Create a template by drawing a 3" (7.5 cm) chili pepper on a piece of paper. Use it as a template, and cut out 6 to 8 chili peppers from the flashing. Paint the chili portion red and the stems green. Let dry.

3. Photocopy and decoupage the Dia de los Muertos image. Affix the chilies slightly underneath the wood with industrial-strength craft glue.

4. Flip the tray over, paint the bottom black, and line it with felt. Cover the entire tray with three coats of varnish. Let dry before using.

TIP Make sure each layer is completely dry before moving on to the next step.

VARIATIONS Use more rope, and leave an extended area on each side to serve as handles for the tray. Create matching mugs by using porcelain paints. Repeat the pattern on the mugs, and bake according to the manufacturer's directions. Use as a charger for each place setting. Set a clear plate on top so the image shows through before the meal is served. If you prefer another theme, paint or decoupage a different image onto the wooden circle.

Artist: Kelly Hale
Dimensions: 12" (30.5 cm) round

Mexican Margarita Candles

You don't have to drink margaritas to enjoy them. This illuminated project is proof of that (no pun intended). These sparkling candles provide an alcohol-free way to enhance your South-of-the-Border theme. If you happen to be serving the real thing, make sure to keep these away from the frosty pitcher.

Materials

ᴪ 2 large glass Mexican margarita glasses

ᴪ 2 wicks, 4" (10 cm) each

ᴪ Piece of paper, 8" x 10" (20.5 cm x 25.5 cm)

ᴪ Yellow candle wax

ᴪ Candle scent (optional)

ᴪ Multicolored star glitter

ᴪ Multicolored loose glitter

ᴪ Acrylic paints in assorted colors

ᴪ White glue

ᴪ Liner brush

ᴪ Oven mitts

ᴪ Double boiler

Makes two candles

1. Clean and thoroughly dry the glasses. Insert a wick in the center of each glass so that the bottom rests just above the stem.

2. In a double boiler, melt the wax over low heat. Add scent drops, if desired.

3. Slowly pour the wax into each glass, filling to ⅛" (3 mm) from the top. Adjust the wicks, if needed. Let the candles sit 10 minutes, and then sprinkle the star glitter onto the wax.

4. After the wax has completely set, pour a small pile of the loose glitter onto a piece of paper. Use your finger to run a line of white glue around the rim of the glass. Dip the glass rim into the glitter one section at a time until the entire top is covered.

4. Use a liner brush to add colored paint to the glass. Brush on the water-based varnish over the paint to preserve your work.

VARIATION Use this application on any kind of drinkware, such as wine glasses or coffee mugs.

Artist: Kathy Cano-Murillo
Dimensions: 7" × 6" (18 cm × 15 cm)

Festive Papier-Mâché Skull

For those who honor El Día de los Muertos (Day of the Dead) on November 1 and 2, a home altar or decorated gravesite is a must. It is believed that on these days the spirits of our dearly departed loved ones return to their homes for one more family fiesta. Who can blame them? One of the main elements in decorating for this happy holiday is to put out a sweet offering of a calaca (sugar skull) adorned with swirls of icing and dots of sequins. For the sake of preserving teeth in the afterlife, here's a boney papier-mâché alternative to the original edible version. What it lacks in calories it makes up for in personality.

Materials

- Balloon
- Glass bowl
- Papier-mâché mix: 2 cups of flour, 1 cup of water, ½ cup of white craft glue
- Piece of cardboard, 6" x 2" (15 cm x 5 cm)
- Newspaper
- Masking tape
- Assorted acrylic paints
- Dimensional squeeze paint
- Loose glitter
- High-gloss varnish
- Paintbrushes
- Scissors

TIPS For cooler climates, drying time may be longer. Also, don't be disappointed if your skull comes out looking less than perfect. The beauty of this project is that each one comes out unique.

Makes one skull

1. Mix the papier-mâché ingredients in a glass bowl until they form a thin pancake-batter consistency. Add extra water or glue if necessary. Tear a newspaper into strips measuring approximately 4" × 2" (10 cm x 5 cm).

2. Blow up the balloon. Cover the entire surface with three layers of papier-mâché. To do this, dip a strip of paper in the mix, remove the excess paste with your fingers, and place the strip on the balloon. Smooth out any bubbles with your fingertips. Coat the balloon with one layer, and begin a second layer on the driest area of the first layer. Follow with a third layer.

3. When the balloon is completely dry, turn it so the pointed end is facing forward. Tape the cardboard directly below the point. Use the blade of the scissors to cut out two circles for the eyes—this will pop the balloon as well—and a triangle for the nose.

4. Add two layers of papier-mâché to cover the eyes and nose, but keep them indented. At the same time, cover the cardboard until the entire skull is formed. Let the skull dry overnight.

5. Apply a basecoat and embellish the skull in desired colors. Paint two rows of teeth on the cardboard area. Add glitter, squeeze paint, rhinestones, or fabric to give your skull personality. Spray with a high-gloss varnish.

VARIATIONS Adjust the size of your skull by using smaller balloons. Have fun by adding false eyelashes, earrings, flowers, or a hat to your *calaca*.

Artist: Kathy Cano-Murillo and Patrick Murillo
Dimensions: 8" × 6" (20.5 cm × 15 cm)

Lucha Libre Place-Card Holders

America has The Rock, but Mexico has El Santo. We're talking wrestling rings and mano y mano combat. Lucha Libre (Mexican wrestling) is a wildly popular South-of-the-Border sport that was launched during the 1930s and has spread worldwide. With names such as El Santo, Mil Mascaras, and the Blue Demon, these comical characters donned ornate and flamboyant costumes that represented a personalized theme. Their style combined the elements of wicked wrestling, circus acrobats, and outlandish audience confrontations. It wasn't long before the success of Lucha Libre spilled over into the arena of the Mexican cinema. These muscled masked men suddenly became more than fighters in a ring; they became cultural icons and superheroes for la gente (the people). Add a bit of that Lucha Libre power to your next party table setting by creating these place-card holders that really pack a punch.

Materials

- ♥ 1 piece of wood, 2" x 3" (5 cm x 7.5 cm)
- ♥ 1 Mexican toy wrestler action figure
- ♥ One 8" (20.5 cm) piece of wire (18 gauge)
- ♥ 2 pieces of thin ribbon, 12" (30.5 cm) each
- ♥ 4 toothpicks
- ♥ 4 beads, ¼" (6 mm) in diameter
- ♥ Paint and paintbrushes or glitter pens
- ♥ Cardstock
- ♥ Markers
- ♥ Glue
- ♥ Needle-nosed pliers
- ♥ Hand drill
- ♥ Scissors
- ♥ Hot glue gun

Makes one place-card holder

1. Drill a hole at each corner of the wood. Snip the pointy ends off of the toothpicks, add a small dollop of glue to one end, and insert them into the holes. Paint the wooden base and the toothpicks, and let dry.

2. Tie one of the ribbon strands to the bottom of one of the toothpicks. Wrap the ribbon around the other toothpicks to create the look of wrestling ring ropes. Repeat the process for the upper ropes, and tie off the ribbon.

3. Decorate the action figure with the paint or glitter pens, let dry, and then glue him slightly off-center in the ring.

4. Use the needle-nosed pliers to create a spiral at the end of the wire. Drill a hole into the wooden base near the feet of the action figure. Add a dollop of hot glue to the wire, and insert it into the hole.

5. Use hot glue to attach the beads on the bottom of the base to act as feet. Decorate the place card with the markers, and insert it into the standing spiral.

VARIATIONS Make your place setting an equal opportunity one. Transform the male wrestlers into female ones by adding long hair and skirts. For an interactive party game, have your guests make up Mexican wrestler names for each other and write them on the back of the place cards.

Artist: Kathy Cano-Murillo
Dimensions: 3" × 5" (7.5 cm × 12.5 cm)

Loteria Glass Charms

Hmmm, which one is mine? After a few sips of high-voltage sangria, it's easy to forget where you've set your glass. No worries here, as long as preparations are made in advance. These wonderful wire glass charms are decorated with miniature laminated images from Loteria (Mexican bingo) game cards. They are then trimmed with beautiful crystal beads. Delicate and dainty, they still make a bold statement about your drinking decor.

Materials

ψ 24-gauge sterling-silver wire, 12" (30.5 cm) long

ψ 4 *Loteria* bingo cards

ψ 8 jump rings

ψ Head pin

ψ Assorted colored glass beads

ψ Empty film canister

ψ Needle-nosed pliers

ψ Safety pin

ψ Scissors

Makes four glass charms

1. Cut the wire into four 3" (7.5 cm) pieces. Wrap each piece around the empty film canister to create a uniformly round shape.

2. Use the needle-nosed pliers to create the clasp and hook for the charms. At one end of each wire, create a small round loop for the clasp, and at the opposite end, bend the wire to make a small hook.

3. At a local copy center, reduce the bingo cards on a color copier to measure 1" (2.5 cm) tall (approximately 75% of full size), and then have them laminated. Cut out the laminated bingo cards. Poke a hole at the top and bottom of each one with the safety pin.

4. Thread 2 or 3 beads on the head pin, and attach it to the jump ring. Then attach the jump ring to the bingo card using the needle-nosed pliers. Attach another jump ring at the top of the bingo card to connect it to the silver wire.

VARIATION Substitute other photos for the bingo cards, if desired.

Artist: Kelly Hale
Dimensions: 2" (5 cm)

Furnishings

For art lovers, scoring distinctive furnishings is as competitive as Olympic competition. For each person searching for the perfect retro, fringed table lamp, another is crying over less-than-stellar sofa pillows. What's a daring decorator to do?

Sure, scouring neighborhood thrift stores, rummage sales, and salvage lots will offer a treasure trove of makeover subjects, but there's an even better way to beat the odds in the design game: Do it yourself!

Don't let the thought intimidate you. You won't have to break a sweat or think too hard to pull off the whimsical furnishing ideas in this chapter. Most only involve paint, a few nails, a staple gun, and decoupage (a little Latin jazz in the background doesn't hurt, either). By the time you reach the last step, you'll be proudly blowing the smoke off the tip of your glue gun. Just the Crazy for Carmen Miranda Lamp on page 78 alone will have your guests gasping in fruity delight. Not to mention the Bossa Nova Barstool on page 80 that may make your creative counterparts green with DIY envy.

The bottom line is you'll have created a functional masterpiece that is true championship style for your home.

Crazy for Carmen Miranda Lamp

She was loud and campy and loved big chunky shoes, gaudy jewelry, and— most of all—wearing fruit on her head. Oh, how we adore her. During the 1940s, this Brazilian bombshell singer and dancer breathed new life into Broadway and Hollywood and gave a new level of respect to fruit. To this day, the name of Carmen Miranda induces toothy smiles and a swivel in the hips. Here's a way to let her spunky spirit brighten up your life and living space. This dimensional desk lamp is oozing with fun and flair. Hats off to Carmen!

Materials

- Ψ 1 black lamp, 24" tall (61 cm)
- Ψ 1 square lamp shade, 8" x 10" (20.5 cm x 25.5 cm)
- Ψ 2 color-copy images of Carmen Miranda
- Ψ Round bead, ½" (1.3 cm) in diameter
- Ψ Yellow tassel, 3" (7.5 cm) long
- Ψ Acrylic paint in fuchsia, lime green, lemon yellow, lilac, and black
- Ψ Fruit-shaped rubber stamps
- Ψ Dimensional squeeze paint
- Ψ Miniature plastic fruit
- Ψ Strings of beads
- Ψ Lime green ruffled trim
- Ψ Beaded fringe
- Ψ White glue
- Ψ Hot glue gun
- Ψ Spray varnish
- Ψ Scissors
- Ψ Assorted paintbrushes

Makes one lamp

1. Apply a basecoat on the lamp shade in assorted colors. Cut out the two Carmen Miranda images, and attach them to opposite sides of the shade using the white glue. Add a bead of squeeze paint around the edges of the image to seal it. On the remaining two sides, apply fruit designs with rubber stamps, and accent them with a liner brush and black paint.

2. Use hot glue to trim the top and the bottom of the shade with the green ruffle. Finish off by adding a row of beads and beaded fringe.

3. Add embellishments to the bottom of the lamp base with paint and the miniature fruit pieces.

4. String the ½" (1.3 cm) bead through the lamp's pull chain, and attach the tassel.

5. Lightly spray the entire lamp with varnish.

VARIATIONS Use four different pictures of Carmen Miranda on the shade, or create a collage by using a variety of pictures.

Artist: Kathy Cano-Murillo
Dimensions: 24" (61 cm)

Bossa Nova Barstool

That sexy bossa nova beat can be oh-so-soothing to the soul and addictive to the feet and hips. But after ever-so-suavely dancing the night away to exotic Brazilian samba rhythms, there comes a point when even the best of partiers needs a little rest. Let this swanky barstool come to the rescue. It's more than just comfy and colorful—it's downright cool.

Materials

- 24" (61 cm) wooden barstool
- ½ yard (46 cm) of oilcloth
- Round seat cushion, 12" (30.5 cm) in diameter, 2" (5 cm) thick
- 1 yard (91.5 cm) of black ball trim
- Assorted acrylic paints
- Spray varnish
- Spray adhesive
- Hammer and gold-colored tacks
- Staple gun
- Hot glue gun
- Scissors
- Sandpaper
- Paintbrushes

Makes one barstool

1. Lightly sand the barstool. Paint a basecoat in the desired colors, and add accents in contrasting colors. Let dry. Spray on three coats of varnish, letting each one dry before the next one is applied.

2. Spray a generous layer of adhesive to the seat's surface and to one side of the cushion. Carefully set the cushion on the seat, making sure it is even. Trim any excess with scissors.

3. Lay out the oilcloth face down on a table. Turn the barstool upside down, and place it on the cloth. Pull one side up underneath the seat area, and staple. Continue the process until the cloth is tightly bound underneath the seat.

4. Flip the barstool over and attach the black ball trim around the rim of the seat with hot glue. Hammer in the tacks to make it more secure.

TIP Use hot glue to keep the cloth tightly in place as you staple it.

VARIATIONS Replace the oilcloth with another type of strong fabric, such as a Mexican blanket or other vinyl covering. Use leftover oilcloth to make drink coasters that match the barstools. Simply glue the fabric to 4" x 4" (10 cm x 10 cm) ceramic tiles or wooden pieces, and add felt tabs to the bottom to protect tabletops. Instead of covering a barstool, use this technique on chairs or ottomans.

Artist: Kathy Cano-Murillo
Dimensions: 24" × 12" (61 cm × 30.5 cm)

Mexican Cinema End Table

There's nothing that can compare to the golden age of Mexican cinema. From 1936 to 1957, Mexico released dozens of fabulously frivolous titles that starred an array of sexy starlets and dashing leading men. Much like Hollywood, the subject matter was as diverse as a combo party platter. There were campy horror flicks, heavyhearted dramas, whodunit mysteries, gaudy musicals, and mythical epics. Many are being rereleased on DVD and video for a whole new generation to enjoy. What better way to watch these pictures than to rest your glass tumbler and popcorn bowl on this embellished end table? It's lined with post-cards that were made from vintage posters, accented with shiny gems, and topped with glass to protect against messy spills. Now, where's that remote control?

Materials

- Ψ 1 square end table, 22" x 22" (56 cm x 56 cm)
- Ψ 20 Mexican cinema postcards
- Ψ 1 piece of glass with sealed edges, 22" x 22" x ½" (45.5 cm x 45.5 cm x 1.3 cm)
- Ψ Gold paint pen
- Ψ Acrylic paint in black and yellow
- Ψ 1 bottle of red squeeze glitter
- Ψ Assorted gems
- Ψ White craft glue
- Ψ Water-based brush-on polyurethane varnish
- Ψ Scissors
- Ψ Paintbrushes

Makes one end table

1. Trim the white edges off of each postcard. Lay out two even rows of five cards on both sides of the table. Starting from the outer edges, brush a layer of white craft glue on the back of a card, and press it in place. Make a fist and rub the cards to make sure all the edges are secured. Apply the remaining cards, ensuring they are all kept in an even order. Outline each card with the gold paint pen.

2. Decorate each leg by adding paint and gluing on gems in a random design. Fill in with hand-drawn swirls with the gold paint pen.

3. Use the paint pen to write different movie titles around the border of the table. Accent with the squeeze glitter, and let dry.

4. Carefully place the glass on top of the table to protect the images underneath.

TIP If you don't want to use the actual postcards, make color copies. If possible, remove the table legs while making this project.

VARIATIONS Line the table with Latin-themed wrapping paper or one large movie poster instead of postcards. Frame the postcards and hang them to match the table.

Artist: Kathy Cano-Murillo
Dimensions: 22" × 22" × 18" (56 cm × 56 cm × 45.5 cm)

Manic Hispanic Canvas Painting

Ancient masks meet modern art in this bold and crisp painting. It adds a whole new medium to the world of mask collecting because this piece is one-dimensional, yet layered with design. This project is for the Latin art aficionados who don't mind adding a contemporary twist to a traditional medium.

Materials

- Ψ 1 primed canvas, 16" x 20" (40.5 cm x 51 cm)
- Ψ Template on page 123
- Ψ Black Sharpie pen
- Ψ Acrylic paints in bronze, red, yellow, green, blue, purple, and orange
- Ψ Gold paint pen
- Ψ Black tracing chalk
- Ψ Ruler
- Ψ Scissors
- Ψ Paintbrushes

Makes one painting

1. Use the ruler and black chalk to divide the canvas into four even quadrants.

2. At a local copy center, make a copy of the template on page 123, and then trace the lines with the chalk. Flip it over, and place it on one quadrant of the canvas. Rub the lines so the design will transfer. Repeat the process for the remaining three quadrants.

3. Paint the backgrounds of each quadrant in contrasting colors.

4. Paint the faces in bronze. Before painting the rest of the masks, use the black Sharpie pen to draw different types of patterns on the headdresses. Finish filling in with color.

5. When the paint is dry, outline the lines and borders with the black Sharpie pen. Use the gold paint pen to add accents where needed.

TIP Make sure the paint is completely dry before outlining with the marker.

VARIATIONS Instead of one large canvas, use four small ones with one mask on each one. For a starker look, use only black and white, or use patina paints for a more rustic style. Expand the concept by using the Aztec calendar in two of the quadrants.

Artist: Kathy Cano-Murillo
Dimensions: 16" × 20" (40.5 cm × 51 cm)

Tamale Oja Wreath

Tamales are one of the main staples of Mexican food — especially around the holiday season. From soaking the ojas (corn husks) and shredding the meat, to peeling the chilies and mixing the masa (corn-based dough), they are also one of the most fun to make. But not everyone can be a champion tamale maker. That's the idea that triggered the next best thing — a tamale art piece! This savvy Southwest-style wreath uses dried ojas as its foundation and dried chilies as the final touch. For crafty types, it's the perfect alternative to the tamale-making mayhem — no soaking, shredding, mixing, or peeling required.

Materials

- One 10" (25.5 cm) straw wreath
- 1 bag of cornhusks
- 2–3 dried red chilies
- 12" (30.5 cm) of Guatemalan ribbon, 1" (2.5 cm) wide
- String or wire
- 1 box of straight pins
- Hot glue gun

Makes one wreath

1. Break apart the cornhusks into single sheets. Take one husk at a time, and fold it gently in half. Lay it the center of the wreath, and insert a straight pin through it to hold it in place.

2. Apply the next husk in the same fashion, except attach it ½" (1.3 cm) lower than the previous one. Repeat the process until you have a row that lies evenly in the inner circle.

3. Repeat the process in the opposite direction for the front of the wreath. Continue to the outside of the wreath, again going in the opposite direction.

4. Wrap two or three dried chilies together at the stem, and tie the group to a string. Tie a knot at the top of the string, and pin it to the top of the front of the wreath. Tie a bow with the ribbon, and hot glue it on top of the string to hide it.

TIP Each husk will take two pins to fully secure it in place. Do not use husks that come from a bag that has been open for more than a week, because they will be too dry to use and will split when the pin is inserted.

VARIATIONS If desired, replace the ribbon with raffia and dried chilies with imitation ones. Split the husks down the center, and use a 6" (15 cm) wreath for a smaller version.

Artist: Kathy Cano-Murillo
(concept by Kim MacEachern)
Dimensions: 12" round (30.5 cm)

El Sol Wall Shelf

In all cultures, the sun is one of the most powerful forces of the cycle of life. But the automatic routine of sunrises and sunsets are often taken for granted because of our busy lifestyles and responsibilities. This distressed wall shelf is one small way to show appreciation to el sol (the sun) and the warmth it brings to our bodies, souls, and spirits. The milagros surrounding it offer a message of hope that these beaming rays of light from the sky will never fade.

Materials

- ψ 1 unfinished wall shelf, 22" x 6" (56 cm x 15 cm)
- ψ Painted *Talavera* sun face
- ψ 2 miniature *Talavera* crosses
- ψ 30–40 *milagros*
- ψ 20–25 silver-colored tacks
- ψ Delta brand Liquid Jewels paint in green and yellow
- ψ 2 eye screws
- ψ 2 jump rings
- ψ Saw-toothed picture hanger
- ψ Industrial-strength craft glue
- ψ Small nails and hammer
- ψ Paintbrushes
- ψ Hand drill
- ψ Book

Makes one shelf

1. Distress the shelf by hammering on it and making small grooves. Paint a layer of green paint to the bottom half of the shelf and a layer of yellow to the top. Do not fill in the distressed crevices with paint.

2. Once both layers are dry, apply a coat of yellow to the bottom half of the shelf and green to the top. Focus on filling the crevices with these opposite colors. Let dry.

3. Nail half of the *milagros* to one side of the bottom portion of the shelf and the remaining amount to the other side. Do not put any in the center. (This is where the sun face will go.)

4. On the ridge across and down the shelf, press in a row of tacks. Drill a small hole in each miniature cross, and insert a jump ring through each hole. Add an eye screw to the bottom of each side of the shelf, and then attach a miniature cross to each one.

5. Apply a generous amount of industrial-strength craft glue to the top half of the back of the sun. Press it into place in the center of the shelf. Slide a book underneath the exposed portion of the sun to make it level so it will adhere evenly. Let it dry for 24 hours, and then attach the saw-toothed picture hanger with small nails and hammer.

TIPS If your shelf has decorative brackets, attach the miniature crosses to them instead of eye screws at the bottom of the shelf. Make sure the adhesive is completely cured before hanging the shelf.

VARIATIONS For a smaller piece, use a wooden plaque. Glue the sun in the center and the cross dangling from the bottom. The *Talavera* sun and crosses can be replaced with terra-cotta versions.

Artist: Kathy Cano-Murillo
Dimensions: 22" × 6" (56 cm × 15 cm)

Café Cultura Clock

Keep forgetting when it's time to make the coffee? Maybe this coffee can clock will serve as the perfect reminder. It's just one example of how you can easily change an everyday object into handy, functional artwork. This piece is perfect for the kitchen, providing there is a steamy cup of café con leche (coffee with milk) on the table alongside a plate of warm and chewy pan dulce (Mexican sweet bread) — all signs that it's the perfect time to relax.

Materials

- ψ 1 can of Mexican coffee
- ψ 1 clock mechanism
- ψ AA battery
- ψ 4 round wooden balls
- ψ Hand drill
- ψ Hot glue and glue gun
- ψ File
- ψ Can opener
- ψ Fine tip marker (optional)
- ψ Paint and paintbrushes (optional)

Makes one clock

1. Using the can opener, remove the bottom of the can, and discard it. Empty the can and set the plastic lid aside for later use. File down any sharp edges around the inside rim.

2. Disassemble the clock mechanism, and lay the pieces in the order they are to be assembled.

3. Choose the side of the can that you wish to use, and locate the center point. Use the hand drill to make a small hole that is large enough for the clock mechanism to fit through. Add hot glue to either side of the clock mechanism's casing, and insert it up inside the can so that the centerpiece protrudes through the hole. Add more glue inside the can to keep the clock in place.

4. Add the remaining elements to the clock according to the manufacturer's directions. Insert the battery inside the clock's casing.

5. Glue the four wooden balls to the plastic lid for "feet." Place the lid on the bottom of the can.

TIPS Mark the center area of the can with a fine-tip marker. If the hands are hard to see, paint them in a bright color.

VARIATIONS If you can't find an imported coffee can, create one of your own with paint and stencils. These coffee cans also look great as pencil, hairbrush, or utensil holders.

Artist: Kathy Cano-Murillo
Dimensions: 8" × 4" (20.5 cm × 10 cm)

Talavera Tile Treasure Mirror

Talavera, a form of earthenware that originated in Talavera de la Reina, Spain, in the sixteenth century, is most often created as a white glazed ceramic. There are many theories of how the method began in Mexico. It is widely believed that Spanish monks living in Mexico recruited the Spanish tilemakers to visit them and teach the indigenous people the art in order to decorate the churches in their homeland's style. These days, most Talavera is produced and used throughout Mexico. This tile frame, which combines the beauty of the tiles with small treasures, requires a great deal of patience. The end result? A far-out and fantastically fun piece for your home.

Materials

- Ψ One 8" x 10" x 2½" (20.5 cm x 25.5 cm x 6.5 cm) wooden frame
- Ψ 3 Talavera tiles in assorted colors, 4" x 4" (10 cm x 10 cm)
- Ψ 1 8" x 10" (20.5 cm x 25.5 cm) mirror
- Ψ 3 solid color tiles, 4" x 4" (10 cm x 10 cm)
- Ψ 1 bag of colored marbles or glass pebbles
- Ψ Assorted trinkets such as *milagros*, beads, or charms
- Ψ Acrylic paints in assorted colors
- Ψ Dimensional squeeze paint
- Ψ 1 tube of Liquid Nails adhesive
- Ψ One 5-lb. (2.5 kg) box of dry grout and water
- Ψ Water-based brush-on polyurethane varnish
- Ψ Sandpaper
- Ψ Sponge and paper towels
- Ψ Rubber spatula
- Ψ Safety goggles, paper mask, and rubber gloves
- Ψ Bath towel
- Ψ Hammer
- Ψ Paintbrushes

Makes one mirror

1. Fold the bath towel in half, and place a tile inside. Put on the safety goggles, and hammer the top of the towel so that the tile is broken into small pieces measuring 1" (2.5 cm). Repeat the process for the remaining tiles. Disassemble the wooden frame, and lightly sand it.

2. Glue the tile and trinket pieces to the wood with the adhesive, keeping them approximately ½" (1.3 cm) from each other. Attach rows of marbles as a border around the edges. Let dry for several hours until fully cured.

3. Wearing a paper mask, mix half of the box of grout according to the directions. Add a dash of more grout or water until you have a toothpaste-like consistency. Put on the rubber gloves, and use the spatula to spread the grout evenly over the frame. Use your fingers to get it into the small crevices. Begin with the inner and outer edges, and work your way to the top. After the entire frame is covered, remove any excess grout with the damp sponge. Let the grout dry for several hours until it is solid, and then use a damp paper towel to clean up the edges and remove any dust.

4. Attach more trinkets with glue to fill in blank spaces. Add color accents by outlining the edges of the tiles and the grout areas with acrylics and dimensional squeeze paint. When dry, coat with a layer of polyurethane varnish and enjoy.

TIP Keep all pieces level with each other. You can do this by gluing trinkets on top of the solid-color tiles.

VARIATION Add a few squirts of acrylic paint to the grout while mixing it, to add color to your piece.

Artist: Kathy Cano-Murillo
Dimensions: 14" × 12" (35.5 cm × 30.5 cm)

T-Shirt Toss Pillow

Mention the idea of "Latin-izing" a home, and T-shirts aren't exactly the first thought to come to mind. But in this case, they are the magic ingredient — that is, if you have a fabulous one that you don't mind cutting up. Here's a cheerful way to preserve the color and crispness of the shirt by transforming it into a gorgeous throw pillow for a sofa or bed. The shirts used in these examples have all been lovingly worn throughout the years. Instead of tossing them out, the artist chose this decorative way of recycling them. Her end results are these luxurious, textured pillows trimmed in ribbon and tassels. Featured on these examples are Adelita, a famous female icon of the Mexican Revolution, the Virgin of Guadalupe, and a Dia de los Muertos version of the "See No Evil/Speak No Evil/Hear No Evil" trio. Now, doesn't this just make you want to go clean out your closet?

Materials

- Ψ 14" x 14" (35.5 cm x 35.5 cm) pillow form
- Ψ ½ yard x ½ yard (46 cm x 46 cm) of printed fabric, washed and ironed
- Ψ Screen-printed cotton T-shirt, washed
- Ψ 1 yard (91.5 cm) of decorative cording
- Ψ Batting
- Ψ Thread and needle
- Ψ Embroidery thread and needle (optional)
- Ψ Velcro strip
- Ψ 15" x 15" (38 cm x 38 cm) square paper pattern
- Ψ 15" x 9" (38 cm x 23 cm) rectangular paper pattern
- Ψ Scissors
- Ψ Sewing machine
- Ψ Iron

TIP Allow extra margins for fabrics that unravel easily or that will need an edge-finishing overcast stitch.

Makes one pillow

1. For the front panel of the pillow, set the 15" × 15" (38 cm × 38 cm) pattern on top of the fabric and cut. Repeat the process for the back panel, but use the 15" × 9" (38 cm × 23 cm) pattern, and cut two pieces.

2. Cut out the centerpiece design from the front of the T-shirt, leaving ½" (1.3 cm) of fabric around the edge to turn under. Baste the batting and the centerpiece in place on the pillow top, turning under the raw edges. If desired, quilt with embroidery thread through all layers for three-dimensional effect.

3. Baste and machine-stitch the trim.

4. Turn under ¼" (6 mm) on the shorter edge of one back panel, and repeat the process on the corresponding panel. Fold 1¼" (3 cm) on each of these finished edges, and press with a hot iron. Baste decorative cording on one panel edge, and machine-stitch in place. Cut and baste the Velcro strip, and sew in place. Cut and baste the fuzzy side of a Velcro strip, on the right side of the corresponding panel's finished edge. Baste and sew in place. Place Velcro strips together to close. Panels should form a 15" square (38 cm).

5. Sew the front and back pillow panels together at all four sides of the seams. Open the Velcro strips and turn the pillowcase right side out. Slip the pillow form inside through the opening.

VARIATIONS These pillows can be made without the use of batting. Printed bandanas can be substituted for T-shirts. Decorate your pillow as mellow or extreme as you like. Use different types of fabrics, such as chenille or velvet, for different looks.

Artist: Anita Y. Mabante Leach
Dimensions: 14" × 14" (35.5 cm × 35.5 cm)

Personal Accessories

In this bustling world, just about everyone can appreciate the value of personal space. That's because it's *muy sagrado*—very sacred. The only objects we allow within our inner circle are those personal accessories that are near and dear to our hearts.

The fascination with these treasures is truly in the eye of the beholder. Sure it sounds a bit syrupy, but don't break out the melodramatic *balada* (ballad) just yet. Personal accessories aren't always seriously sentimental. Think of that crazy *tia* (aunt) who can't get enough of her hot-pink flamingo brooch, or the co-worker who has her desk covered with kooky clippings. These are just two examples of how much fun it is when our personal space overflows into our personal style.

Accessories can include one-of-a-kind jewelry pieces that are worn faithfully each day, vintage family photos on a fireplace mantle, and even yummy scented candles. Together or separately, they are some of life's little ingredients that reflect our moods and define our personalities. This is where handcrafted mementos fit in. They are designed as a form of expression with the good intention to inspire or humor.

The following pages are all about constructing a dashing collection of Latin-tinged keepsakes. There are plenty of diverse accessories to make for yourself, plus extras to be shared with cherished *compañeros*. Some, such as the Stained-Glass Prayer Candle on page 104 and the Wood-Burned Retablo on page 102, are meant for reflective purposes, such as prayer altars or curios, whereas others like the Mariachi Tote Bag on page 108 and the Novela Note Cards on page 112 are strictly for playful fun and quirky camp.

Bottle Cap Pebble Pins

Bottle caps—they aren't just for popping off anymore. In the art universe, they've become a crafty tool for creating everything from jewelry to tambourines. If you are new to these ruffled tin tops, here is a great introduction to get your creative juices fizzing—just like all the soda you'll have to drink in order to collect the bottle caps!

Materials

- Ψ Bottle cap
- Ψ Clear glass pebble
- Ψ Small image
- Ψ Loose glitter
- Ψ Assorted acrylic paints
- Ψ *Milagro* charm
- Ψ Tin
- Ψ Jump ring
- Ψ Pin back
- Ψ Industrial-strength craft glue
- Ψ White glue
- Ψ Hand drill
- Ψ Paintbrushes
- Ψ Scissors

Makes one pin

1. Drill a hole in the edge of the bottle cap.

2. Trim the image so that it fits under the glass pebble. Apply a dab of white glue to the flat side of the pebble, and adhere it to the image. Smooth out any air bubbles with your finger, and let dry.

3. Add a small dollop of industrial-strength craft glue to the back of the pebble, and insert it in the center of the bottle cap. Press it firmly in place, and let dry. Cover the surrounding inside area of the bottle cap with paint, and then sprinkle on the loose glitter.

4. Slide the jump ring through the hole, and attach the *milagro* charm so that it dangles.

5. Cut a piece of tin to serve as the background for the bottle cap, and glue the bottle cap in place. Attach the pin back with industrial-strength craft glue.

TIP Do not use frosted or colored glass pebbles, because the picture will not show through clearly.

VARIATIONS This project also works wonderfully to make magnets or necklaces. Make multiple bottle caps to line a picture frame or the border of a coffee table.

Artist: Kathy Cano-Murillo
Dimensions: 2½" × ½" (6.5 cm × 1.3 cm)

Crazy Calaca Jewelry Set

Día de los Muertos is all about frivolity and flair. On this beloved holiday, nothing can be too outlandish or too wild. This jewelry sets the tone for the festivities to come. It is tightly packed with an arousing array of multicolored and ethnic beads, charms, and handmade miniature calaca (skeleton) heads that glow with mischievous glee. This project is a bit on the tedious side, but offers a chance to joyfully reflect on the lives of those who have touched our hearts. And just like our memories, this set is welcome year-round.

Materials

ψ Assorted beads and charms

ψ Assorted colored seed beads

ψ 1 silver chain bracelet with clasp

ψ 1 yard (91.5 cm) black ribbon

ψ White oven-bake clay

ψ 2 fishhook earrings

ψ Black acrylic paint

ψ 35–40 jump rings, ⅜" (1 cm)

ψ Head and eye pins

ψ Glue

ψ Water-based brush-on polyure-thane varnish

ψ Needle-nosed pliers

ψ Ballpoint pen

ψ Tin snips

TIPS For the earrings, only use lightweight beads. Make sure the jump rings are tightly closed; otherwise, the head and eye pins will fall through.

Makes one bracelet, necklace, and earring set

1. Pull off a pea-sized piece of clay, and press it between your fingers to make a circle. To make the skulls, pinch the bottom of the circle to form a square jaw. With a ballpoint pen, make two holes for the eyes, an upside-down V for the nose, and lines for the teeth. Use a head pin to poke a hole at the top of the skull. Repeat the process to make 15 skulls, and bake them according to the manufacturer's directions. Let cool, and then dip a head pin in the black paint, and fill in the holes you made with the ballpoint pen. Let them dry, and brush on a layer of varnish.

2. On a head pin, thread one bead sandwiched between two seed beads. Snip the excess from the pin. Set aside, and repeat the process until you have 20 beaded head pins. Make another set using the eye pins.

3. To incorporate the clay skulls, snip 15 of the eye pins down to 1" (2.5 cm) long. Add a dab of glue at the end of the pins, and insert them through the hole at the top of the skull. An eyehole will protrude from the top of each skull. Attach these skulls as danglers for your jewelry pieces.

4. With the needle-nosed pliers, attach the head pins to the eye pins and then to a jump ring at the top. Lay the bracelet out flat, and arrange the beaded pieces below it to create an appealing and balanced pattern. Once you find a pattern you like, use the pliers to attach the pieces.

5. To make the earrings, make two sets of three beaded head and eye pins. Attach them to the fishhook earrings.

6. To make the necklace, repeat the process using six sets. After attaching the jump rings with the beaded head and eye pins, thread the ribbon though. Tie a knot at both ends to secure.

VARIATION To make a choker necklace, shorten the length of the ribbon and use fewer beads. For a less busy bracelet, use fewer pieces and no eye pins. Replace the bracelet chain with thick elastic cording.

Artist: Kathy Cano-Murillo
Dimensions: 7" × 1½" (18 cm × 4 cm)

Wood-Burned Retablo

Retablos have been a prominent aspect of Latin culture long before the ninteenth century. Originating in Spain and derived from the Latin term retro tabula (behind the altar), they have been created by hand in many forms: from tin to wood, from simple to elaborate. Retablos are known for their beautiful images of patron saints or other types of pictures of devotion. They are used in a multitude of places for a variety of reasons. Many spiritual people and families use them as adornments in home altars, and others share them with loved ones at public memorials. It is believed that having a retablo or two within your environment will bring peace, happiness, good health, love, and prosperity.

Materials

- Ψ 2 pieces of pine
- Ψ Wood-burning utensil
- Ψ 1 small hinge with screws
- Ψ Assorted wood-stain markers or acrylic paints
- Ψ Jigsaw
- Ψ Sandpaper
- Ψ Screwdriver

Makes one *retablo*

1. Use a jigsaw to cut out the wooden pieces, and then join them with the hinge. Sand the edges smooth.

2. Using the wood-burning utensil, draw a design or image onto the front and back of the wood.

3. Use wood-stain markers or paint to color in the shapes or to add words or borders.

TIPS Use transfer paper if you would like to use a picture instead of drawing freehand. Enlarge the template to create larger wood shapes for your *retablo.*

VARIATION This concept can be used on larger wooden objects, such as jewelry boxes, wall hangings, or tabletops.

Artist: Patrick Murillo
Dimensions: 4" × 5" (10 cm × 12.5 cm)

Stained-Glass Prayer Candle

In Latin culture, altars and shrines are common fare and are often assembled in the home for a variety of reasons, such as to celebrate Día de los Muertos, to honor a loved one, to enhance meditation, and to channel positive energy. Prayer candles are vital to these sacred spaces. They come in dozens of different designs, usually adorned with beautiful images of saints. Recently, modern artists have embellished them with pop culture icons and whimsical themes. Regardless of the style, the meaning is universal. The eternal flame represents life and hope. Just as each altar is as original as the person who created it, these hand-painted stained-glass candles follow suit.

Materials

ψ 1 tall prayer candle

ψ 1 bottle of simulated leading

ψ Assorted colors of Gallery Glass paint

ψ Small paintbrush

ψ Loose glitter

ψ Rhinestones

ψ Dry-erase marker

Makes one candle

1. Plan your design on a piece of paper, and then draw it on the candle with the dry-erase marker.

2. Outline the design with the simulated leading, and let dry for four hours.

3. Fill in the areas with desired Gallery Glass colors, and let dry. If color is too transparent, apply a second coat.

4. Accent the design with loose glitter and rhinestones.

TIP If you want to use a specific design, place the design under a sheet of clear plastic and trace over it with the simulated leading. After the leading dries, fill it in with the Gallery Glass paint. Let it dry, and then carefully peel the completed design from the clear sheet and apply it to the candle.

VARIATION Use this same process on glass vases or cookie jars.

Artist: Kathy Cano-Murillo
Dimensions: 8½" × 3" (21.5 cm × 7.5 cm)

Divine Intervention Car Cross

Need protection from road rage? Hanging this sprightly, swinging car ornament on your rearview mirror just might help. Not only does it look fabulous, it also serves double duty. It's equipped with shiny elastic cording and a lovely bottle cap image that faces outward to thwart off everything from drunk drivers to falling rocks to moose-crossing signs. From inside your car, it's a safeguard against backseat drivers, food spills, or really bad music. Think of how safe our roads would be if everyone had a little divine intervention dangling around.

Materials

- Ψ 2 Popsicle sticks
- Ψ 2 bottle caps, each with a favorite image glued in the center
- Ψ 6 different colors of ribbon
- Ψ Metallic pipe cleaners
- Ψ Squeeze glitter
- Ψ 22-gauge wire
- Ψ Hot glue gun

Makes one car cross

1. Wrap the Popsicle sticks in layers of contrasting colors of ribbon, and secure with hot glue. Glue the two sticks together to make a cross.

2. Twist the wire around the cross to add an accent. Cover the tips of the sticks with squeezable glitter.

3. On one side, tie a bow using a strand of ribbon, and affix it to the center of the cross. Line the outside of the bottle cap with the pipe cleaner, and glue the cap on top of the bow.

4. Flip the cross over, and repeat the process.

5. Glue on a piece of ribbon for hanging.

TIP Seal your picture inside the bottle cap with varnish or resin.

VARIATIONS Make a larger cross for inside your home. Use yarn if you don't have ribbon. Use other objects for the center of the cross if you don't want a bottle cap. Hang a tassel at the bottom of the cross for a bolder look. Add a suction cup to hang it from a back window.

Artist: Goldie Garcia
Dimensions: 8" × 4½" (20.5 cm × 11.5 cm)

Flashy Flamenco Box

Elegant, flamboyant, mesmerizing, and breathtaking—these are qualities that make flamenco style the respected and beloved art it is today. With castanets in hand, gorgeous Spanish women decked out in tiered, ruffled lace skirts, chunky black heels, bolero brims, and oversized hoop earrings sure know how to keep the Mediterranean Latin spirit alive. But flamenco music and dance is much more than meets the eye. Its exotic and emotional energy soothes the soul by way of eloquent guitar melodies, romantic vocals, and heart-pounding lyrics, accompanied by the sharp feet stamping, hand clapping, skirt flipping, and tricky twirls. If visiting Spain (or a local flamenco show) isn't on your current agenda, why not assemble a keepsake box such as this? This wooden jewelry case is overflowing with lace, mirrors, and flowers in an attempt to capture a bit of that Spanish vigor and vitality. To that, we say Ole!

Materials

- Wooden jewelry box, 12" x 4" (30.5 cm x 10 cm)
- 1½ yards (1.5 m) of black lace
- 22" (56 cm) black ball trim
- 2 flamenco coasters or pictures
- 4" x 6" (10 cm x 15 cm) wooden plaque
- 4 miniature round mirrors
- 4 wood balls, 1" (2.5 cm) in diameter
- Acrylic paints in black, red, white, purple, blue, yellow, and green
- Assorted brushes
- Brush-on water-based polyurethane varnish
- Hot glue gun

Makes one box

1. Apply a basecoat of acrylic paint on the inside of the box (black), the top (red), and the sides (green). Paint the wooden plaque black, and glue one of the coasters or pictures to the center of it. Paint green vines and leaves with yellow, purple, and blue flowers. Varnish it, let it dry, and then affix the black ball trim around the rim.

2. Hot-glue the now-decorated wooden plaque to the center of the jewelry box. Glue a miniature mirror in each corner, and add white dots of acrylic paint around the edges of the mirrors. Create petals around each mirror for accents. Cover the remaining surrounding areas with brush strokes of greenery and flowers. Add rows of dots around the side of the lid and a layer of varnish.

3. Open the box and glue the other coaster or picture inside the lid, and add painted accents around it. Paint the wooden balls, and glue them to the bottom of the box. Varnish the entire box.

4. Close the box, and use hot glue to trim the bottom sides of the box in the black lace.

TIPS Make sure the box is completely dry after each step before moving onto the next. Before gluing the plaque in place, find the center of the box and lightly mark it so you know where to permanently adhere the plaque.

VARIATION For a simpler look, apply the coaster or picture directly to the box without using the plaque. Trim the plaque in the same type of lace as you use on the bottom of the box.

Artist: Kathy Cano-Murillo
Dimensions: 12" × 4" (30.5 cm × 10 cm)

Mariachi Tote Bag

In the past decade, vinyl has been making a comeback in the music industry. But why should the record players have all the fun? Often, the cover art is just as entertaining as its grooved contents. Case in point: vintage Mariachi records. The bold images are bursting with character and campy flair. It would be a shame to stash them in a dusty record collection where they can't be adored and appreciated.

If you can lace a shoe and don't mind making a quick stop at the copy center, this quirky, easy-to-assemble tote bag is calling your name. Whether it's used at the sandy beach to hold a towel and sunscreen or to hold clothes for a casual weekend getaway, carrying this bag around will definitely allow you to arrive in signature style.

Materials

- Ψ 2 record album covers
- Ψ 2 pieces of printed stationery, 6" x 14" (15.2 cm x 35.5 cm)
- Ψ 6 strips of satin cording, 30" (76.2 cm) each
- Ψ 2 strips of satin cording, 14" (35.5 cm) each
- Ψ Hole punch
- Ψ 2 pieces of clear plastic tubing, 1" x 16" (3 cm x 40.6 cm)
- Ψ 1 Mardi Gras necklace with large beads 3/8" (1 cm) round
- Ψ 4 large jump rings, 2" (5 cm) round
- Ψ Colored ribbon
- Ψ Scissors
- Ψ Hot glue gun
- Ψ Clear tape
- Ψ Hole-punch reinforcements

Makes one tote bag

1. At your local copy center, have all your paper laminated. If your albums are thick, have them laminated twice. Trim the laminated edges, leaving a 1/2" (1.3 cm) border all the way around.

2. Starting with a side panel (the printed stationery) and front panel (an album cover), line up the edges evenly. Make sure the image is facing outward. Apply a small piece of tape to hold them in place. Punch a line of holes approximately 1/2" (1.3 cm) apart along the edges of the stationery and album cover.

3. Lace the two pieces together using the satin cording. Continue the process until all four sides are connected. Repeat to attach the bottom.

4. Punch a hole through the plastic tubing 1/2" (1.3 cm) from the end on each end and then two holes on the top of the album covers. Add the hole-punch reinforcements. Thread the Mardi Gras necklace into the tubing, and then connect the handles to the bag with the jump rings.

5. Use a hot glue gun to trim the edges with colored ribbon. Make inward creases in the side panels by pressing the two album cover sides together.

TIPS Use the hot glue gun to seal any open edges of the laminate. For heavy-duty usage, connect the panels with grommets and leather.

VARIATIONS If desired, cut a Guatemalan belt to use as handles instead of tubing, or embellish the outside further with rhinestones and glitter. Create a matching wallet or sunglass case.

Artist: Kathy Cano-Murillo
Dimensions: 14" × 14" × 6"
(35.5 cm × 35.5 cm × 15 cm)

Novela Note Cards

Forbidden love! Ruthless betrayal! Life-or-death secrets of the heart! We're not talking Hollywood movies, but rather. . . .comic books? That's right. Except these cartoon page-turners are not for los niños (the kids), but more for the seasoned culture hound who prefers to walk on the wild side of souvenirs. The printed versions of Mexican novelas (soap operas) are just as hot and racy as the televised ones. Packed with juicy, nail-biting storylines and melodramatic characters, it's no wonder they are one of the most outlandish guilty pleasures of Mexican collectibles. Which is exactly why they work wonderfully as fun and funky note cards — and are sure to induce a giggle or two.

Materials

- Ψ Blank note cards with envelopes
- Ψ Mexican comic book
- Ψ Patterned stationery or metallic adhesive paper
- Ψ Glue stick and hot glue gun
- Ψ Gems (optional)
- Ψ Stickers or fabric trim
- Ψ Scissors
- Ψ Ruler

Makes one note card and envelope

1. Leaf through the comic book to find a vibrant picture, or if the book is black and white, use the color cover page. Trim the excess white border from around the picture

2. Measure and cut a piece of stationery or metallic adhesive paper that is approximately ½" (1.3 cm) larger than the comic book picture. Use the glue stick to adhere it to the image as the background, and then glue the picture in place at an angle or in the center of the card.

3. Add rows of stickers or fabric trim around the picture and, if desired, gems. Maintain the theme by decorating the envelope as well. Cut a small scrap of paper and an image from the comic, and adhere them to one corner of the front of the envelope or as a flap sealer on the back.

TIPS Do not glue anything until you have first practiced different layouts. Work on a flat, clean surface to avoid wrinkling your card. Some comic books can be racy—you can use squeeze glitter or paint to cover cleavage if necessary.

VARIATIONS Create a collage on the front of the card by cutting out a variety of pictures. Use the Mexican horoscopes at the back of the book for an astrological theme. Make an accordion card, and use a series of the comic pictures.

Artist: Kathy Cano-Murillo
Dimensions: 6" × 5" (15 cm × 12.5 cm)

Embroidered Dish Towels

Embroidery, often considered an art form that only nanas (grandmas) were known for, has recently become one of the trendier crafts of the new century. This graceful and delicate process of drawing with thread not only adds a personal touch to sentimental items but also brightens up everyday objects. These dish towels were given a crisp cultural makeover, thanks to some primitive Aztec designs and a little stitch wizardry.

Materials

- ψ 1 dish towel
- ψ DMC 6-strand floss in desired colors
- ψ Template on page 124
- ψ Embroidery hoop
- ψ Embroidery needle
- ψ Fusible interfacing
- ψ Carbon paper and pencil
- ψ Scissors
- ψ Ruler
- ψ Iron

Makes one dish towel

1. Trace the template on page 124 onto the dish towel using the carbon paper and pencil.

2. Position the embroidery hoop over the traced pattern, and screw it in place until the fabric is tight.

3. Cut a 24" (61 cm) strand of one color of the floss. Thread the needle, leaving a 2" (5 cm) strand remaining from the eye. Tie a double knot at the other end, and then embroider the design. Use a split stitch for straight lines, the lazy daisy stitch for the flower petals, and French knots for the dots. Make sure to secure tight knots if the towel will be used frequently.

4. When finished, iron on the fusible interfacing to the back of the designs to prevent unraveling.

TIPS Wash the dish towel before you embroider to prevent the design from shrinking and puckering. Do not wash with fabric softener because it may cause the iron-on interfacing to break down. Keep the pattern along the edge of the towel so it can be used without ruining the needlework.

VARIATIONS Embroider designs on any kind of fabric for any kind of use, such as handkerchiefs, blouses, napkins, scarves, or purses. Make your own dish towel by using 100% cotton pique, cutting it to size, and then hemming the edges.

Artist: Jenny Hart
Dimensions: 12" × 12" (30.5 cm × 30.5 cm)

Templates

The following templates can be used to make several of the projects found in this book. Feel free to use these images for projects of your own. They can be enlarged or reduced on a copy machine to fit your design.

Template for the Fruit Crate Revolutionary Frame
on page 20.

Template for the Zoot Suit Night-light
on page 24.

LA CORONA

EL CORAZON

EL SOL

LAS PALMAS

Templates for the Reverse-Painted Box
on page 30.

Template for the Mirrored Mission Ornaments
on page 34.

Template for the Aztec Cactus Garden
on page 42.

Template for the Manic Hispanic Canvas Painting
on page 84.

Template for the Embroidered Dish Towel
on page 114.

Resources

Amazon.com
Cine Mexicano Postcard Set
Aztec Motif Rubber Stamp Set

Beads Galore
Beads and charms
2123 S. Priest, #201
Tempe, AZ 85282
800-424-9577
www.beadsgalore.com

Cost Plus World Market
Ethnic trinkets
Locations nationwide
www.costplus.com

Dos Mujeres Mexican Folk Art
Loteria bingo cards, imports
www.mexicanfolkart.com

Faustos Gallery
Milagro miracle charms
www.faustosgallery.com

Flamenco Shop
Spanish flamenco coasters and accessories
www.flamencoshop.com

Kelly Hale
Dia de los Muertos devil image from page 66

The Home Depot
Wood, glass, hardware
Locations nationwide
www.homedepot.com

Jo-Ann Fabrics and Crafts
Fabric, trims, and art materials
Locations nationwide
www.joann.com

Mad Chicken Town
Lucha libre action figures, *novela* comic books
602-277-5329
www.madchickentown.com

MexGrocer.com
Mexican soda pop, La Morena jalapeños, El Pato hot
sauce, corn husks, dried chilies, prayer candles
www.mexgrocer.com

Michaels The Arts and Crafts Store
Art materials
www.michaels.com

Pisces Soap
Soap-making materials
369 S. Doheny Dr., #106
Beverly Hills, CA 90211
www.piscessoap.com

Repro Depot Fabrics
917 SW 152nd St.
Burien, WA 98166
www.reprodepotfabrics.com

St. Theresa's Textile Trove
Exotic multicultural patterned fabrics
1329 Main St.
Cincinnati, OH 45210
800-236-2450
www.sttheresatextile.com

Scraps n Stamps
Decorative papers and stamps
1910 W. Northern Ave.
Phoenix, AZ 85021
602-588-0760
www.scrapsnstamps.com

Sublime Stitching
Embroidery kits
www.sublimestitch.com

Sueños
Latin American imports
4200 N. 7th Ave.
Phoenix, AZ 85013
602-265-3486
www.milagromercado.com

Contributors

Michelle Zecchini Cano
P.O. Box 93743
Phoenix, AZ 85070
e-mail: mzcano@cox.net
Michelle Zecchini Cano is an interior designer and artist who lives with her husband David and their little shaggy dog, Bo. This is the third book in which she has contributed her work.

Goldie Garcia
1227 8th St., NW
Albuquerque, NM 87102
505-242-1396
Web site: www.goldiegarcia.com
Goldie Garcia creates a unique line of contemporary art ranging from bottle cap earrings to religious and secular shrines. Her work can be found in the collections of actors Al Pacino, Laura Dern, Julia Roberts, Paul Rodriguez, and Billy Bob Thornton.

Kelly Hale
e-mail: kellyhale55@hotmail.com
Kelly Hale is a visual display designer by day and an artist in his Arizona studio by night.

Jenny Hart
P.O. Box 8345
Austin, TX 78713
e-mail: jenny@sublimestitching.com
Web site: www.sublimestitching.com
Jenny Hart is a multimedia artist who is most known for her hand-stitched embroidery portraits. Her work is carried in galleries and shops from Dallas, Texas, to Seattle, Washington, and several places in between.

Kerith E. Henderson
369 S. Doheny Dr., #106
Beverly Hills, CA 90211
e-mail: piscessoap@aol.com
Web site: www.piscessoap.com
Designer Kerith E. Henderson is the originator of Pisces Soap, a Beverly Hills–based company. Her handcrafted soaps are both fun and functional, blending wildly imaginative ideas with quality ingredients.

Bryant "Eduardo" Holman
e-mail: bryanth@presidiotex.net
Web site: www.ojinaga.com
Bryant "Eduardo" Holman is a multimedia artist who specializes in Mexican-themed wood-carved nichos and frames.

Anita Y. Mabante Leach
e-mail: nitaleach@yahoo.com
Anita Mabante Leach thanks her mother, Alice, for teaching her the basics of needle arts, including sewing, embroidering, crocheting, knitting, and quilting. Anita, whose day job is writing for a newspaper marketing department, sees needle arts as a great way to bring balance into a busy life.

Patrick Murillo
4223 W. Orchid Ln.
Phoenix, AZ 85051
Phone: 623-847-3750
e-mail: patrickmurillo@hotmail.com
Web site: www.chicanofolkart.com
Patrick Murillo is a professional painter, reggae musician, and art teacher who celebrates his Mexican-American culture through his work and lifestyle.

Acknowledgments

La Casa Loca isn't just the title of this book; it's also how my life was during the authoring of it. The dishes piled up, the kids had to sort and fold their own laundry, and my better half learned the graceful art of household multitasking.

It's to my husband and kids that I owe the most gratitude. I'm sure I must have frightened them a few times while I was knee-deep in making the projects for this book—especially the time I was so consumed with creativity that I accidentally mistook a glue stick for lip balm. There were many times when they pulled me away from the art room to treat me to a nice dinner out. Twice they discovered that my hair was highlighted in glitter flecks. No worries, though—they helped me remove it before our waitress noticed.

I'd also like to thank Norma and David Cano (Mom and Dad) and all my family members who helped me in ways both big and small: Theresa Cano, David Cano, Michelle Cano, Susie Murillo, and Stephanie and Patrick Hadley. Much heartfelt appreciation goes out to all my cousins and in-laws for understanding why I had to miss many family gatherings while completing this book.

Honorary glitter glue sticks are reserved for the fabulous contributors who were so kind to lend their crafty talents. Hugs for my friends and coworkers who were always open to hear about *La Casa Loca* updates: Minnie Torres, Laurie Notaro, Michelle Savoy, Kerry Lengel, Mitchell Vantrease, Michelle Craig, Scott Craven, Ben and Jane Gordon, Connie Midey, the Costa Family, the Castillo Family, the crafty *chicas* at GetCrafty.com and Glitter, Gayle Bass, my University of Phoenix learning teams, and the sales clerks at Michaels The Arts and Crafts Store and Jo-Ann Fabrics and Crafts.

I owe eternal thanks to Maren Bingham, Jenny Ignaszewski, Susan Felt, Zada Blayton, and Terri Ouellette for indirectly inspiring my career in writing and crafting! Most of all I'd like to thank my book editor, Mary Ann Hall, and the Rockport Staff.